MW00415275

GOD IS EVERYWHERE!

RECOGNIZING OUR EXTRAORDINARY GOD IN ORDINARY LIFE

BOB JENNERICH

Unless otherwise noted, scripture quotations taken from the (NASB®) New American Standard Bible®, Copyright © 1960, 1971, 1977, 1995, 2020 by The Lockman Foundation. Used by permission. All rights reserved. www.lockman.org

Additional Scriptures Used:

THE HOLY BIBLE, NEW INTERNATIONAL VERSION®, NIV® Copyright © 1973, 1978, 1984, 2011 by Biblica, Inc.® Used by permission. All rights reserved worldwide.

Scripture quotations are from the ESV® Bible (The Holy Bible, English Standard Version®), copyright © 2001 by Crossway, a publishing ministry of Good News Publishers. Used by permission. All rights reserved.

Scripture quotations marked (NLT) are taken from the Holy Bible, New Living Translation, copyright ©1996, 2004, 2015 by Tyndale House Foundation. Used by permission of Tyndale House Publishers, Carol Stream, Illinois 60188. All rights reserved.

Scripture quotations marked HCSB are taken from the Holman Christian Standard Bible®, Used by Permission HCSB ©1999,2000,2002,2003,2009 Holman Bible Publishers. Holman Christian Standard Bible®, Holman CSB®, and HCSB® are federally registered trademarks of Holman Bible Publishers.

Scripture quotations are from Common Bible: New Revised Standard Version Bible, copyright © 1989 National Council of the Churches of Christ in the United States of America. Used by permission. All rights reserved worldwide.

Scripture taken from the New King James Version®. Copyright © 1982 by Thomas Nelson. Used by permission. All rights reserved.

Copyright © 2021 by Bob Jennerich

All rights reserved.

No part of this book may be reproduced in any form or by any electronic or mechanical means, including information storage and retrieval systems, without written permission from the author, except for the use of brief quotations in a book review.

❀ Created with Vellum

ALSO BY BOB JENNERICH

Free Book!

Type this URL to get a free book called This Is God's Plan?! How
We Can Be Certain in Days of Uncertainty.

https://dl.bookfunnel.com/usje1pnyu0

Also Available for sale:

Facing Life's Challenges Head On: How Jesus Gets You Through
What You Can't Get Around

INTRODUCTION

A few months after I was called to pastor Grace Redeemer Community Church, one of the elders suggested that I periodically write an encouraging email to the church body. The devotional thoughts in this book are the result of that suggestion. I tried to write one every week beginning in 2018, but I couldn't keep up with that schedule. I write them when something I see triggers a thought about God, and I have time to put pen to paper, (fingers to keyboard.)

Most of these devotionals fall into one of two categories. Some are about knowing that we have eternal life in Jesus Christ. They focus more on the belief that Jesus died on the cross for our sins and rose from the dead, and that all who believe in Him will be in heaven with Him for eternity. They are what I would call "salvation" devotionals. Others are more geared toward how we live after we've been saved. A Christian is called to follow Jesus. The Biblical word for following Jesus is "Discipleship." So, I would call them "discipleship" devotionals. There are a few that are related to lessons learned during Covid-19 pandemic of 2020-21, which is ongoing as I write.

The goal of each devotional is to simply mention something that I've seen in everyday life, and then use it as a launching point to talk about the glory of God. Pretty simple. I've included 52 of them, one for each week. (Mainly because I haven't written 365 of them to make it a daily devotional!) A week will allow you plenty of time to reflect on each devotional, but obviously, you can read them as quickly or as slowly as you want. I hope you enjoy them enough to read them daily. At the end of each devotional are discussion questions if you are reading this book with a group. If not, I recommend keeping a journal where you can record your thoughts and responses to each question.

It's amazing to me, that if you are looking for God, you truly can see Him everywhere, thus the title of this devotional book. As I've looked back over the devotionals, I'm reminded that God is with me when I'm cooking in my kitchen. He's with me on my daily walks. He's present in the sports and movies I watch. He's in the night sky that I love to gaze upon with wonder. He's on the golf course. He's in my home improvement projects. He's literally everywhere! The fact that God is everywhere is not news. But often we don't take the time to see Him. I pray that as you read these devotional thoughts, you too will learn to see God everywhere. He's as near as can be, and in all you can see.

ABSENT-MINDEDNESS

1 Peter 5:8: "Your adversary the devil prowls around like a roaring lion looking for someone to devour." (NIV)

I WENT TO THE SUPERMARKET THE OTHER DAY, AND AS IS MY (bad) habit, I took the credit card that I planned to use out of my wallet so I wouldn't have to carry my whole wallet around the store. I also picked up some trash from the floor of my car to throw out on the way into the store. I loaded up my cart and proceeded to the check out. I reached into my pocket for my credit card and came out with only lint. I frantically slapped my other pockets. Nothing!

It was then that I realized what I had done. I had tossed my credit card into the trash can with the other garbage from my car! I had to run out to the car to get another credit card, (feeling the weight of the angry scowls of the people waiting to checkout behind me). I ran back in and paid, and then prayed that the credit card was still in the trash can. It was almost empty. I didn't know if that was good or bad. If they had just replaced the bag, I would have had to ask where the dumpster was and who knows what manner of filth I might have had to climb through to get my credit card back.

Thankfully, the garbage bag had not been changed. I was able to retrieve my credit card, suffering only minor embarrassment from the stares of a few people who noticed. But the whole incident got me thinking about how many things we do without ever even thinking or realizing that we do them. How many times have you walked into a room and forgotten why you went in there? Or you weren't paying attention in a store and you bumped right into someone. It happens all the time, usually without great consequence.

But what if we are walking through life *spiritually* absent-minded? That's a much bigger deal. We've been studying 1 Peter in Sunday School in our church lately. Three times in the letter Peter warned his readers to be sober-minded and alert. Then in the last chapter of the letter, after his third warning, he added that "your adversary the devil prowls around like a roaring lion looking for someone to devour." (1 Peter 5:8). Many people go through life spiritually unaware. They don't give much thought to whether God exists, who Jesus is, why He lived and died, or whether He rose from the dead, or what difference it would make if He did. It's just not important to them. They are blissfully unaware, and yet their eternity hangs on their answers to these questions. Satan loves blissfully unaware people.

They are on the road to damnation and they don't even know it.

Other people call themselves Christians, and genuinely seem to care about these questions. They have made professions of faith, and still somehow Satan can cause them to fall into sin. We've all read stories about Christians who yielded to the temptation of sexual sin, or greed, or power, or other sins. Satan loves to cause a believer to stumble. That's why the warning in 1 Peter to be alert against the wiles of the devil is so severe. By the time Peter wrote that letter, Christians were being thrown to the lions in the Roman colosseum. Most people in his time had seen what lions do to people. They would not have missed the gory image. Peter wanted his readers to know that if we are not aware, Satan will do to our souls what lions will do to our bodies.

If we, or people we know, go through life either convinced that Satan doesn't exist, or absent-mindedly assuming that he doesn't, the consequences will be eternal. He will have succeeded in devouring our souls as a lion would devour our bodies. On the other hand, if we trust Jesus for our salvation, the Holy Spirit will give us the power to resist the devil. Now is not the time for spiritual slumber. There is a spiritual battle raging for our souls every day. Satan does not rest. He's working right now, this very second, to hinder people from becoming Christians, and to tempt Christians to ruin their lives through sin. Be aware! Satan is on the prowl, looking to devour them, and you! It's one thing to absent-mindedly throw away a credit card. It's another thing to absent-mindedly allow Satan to have our souls!

REFLECTIONS:

- Recall a time when you did something funny or embarrassing because you weren't paying attention?

- What are some practical ways that you can remind yourself that Satan exists and means you harm?

RESISTING SPIRITUAL DRAG

Luke 2:52: "And Jesus kept increasing in wisdom and stature, and in favor with God and men."

A PROFESSIONAL GOLFER DRIVES A BALL AT 168 MILES PER hour on average. As the ball screams through the air down the fairway, several external pressures work against it to slow it down. The weight of the ball and the force of gravity push the ball down. Another term used in the study of aerodynamics is "drag." It's the resistance that slows an object as it moves through the air. Gravity, weight, and drag will all cause the ball to land. Then friction with the ground combined with these other forces will cause the ball to bounce, then roll, then stop completely. Golf ball manufacturers are constantly trying to invent new ways to help the ball resist the forces of drag and gravity.

The Roman Empire was the largest empire the world had ever seen. It lasted for nearly 1000 years. It started in the 6th century BC, covered all of Italy by the 3rd century BC, and expanded to its greatest breadth by the 2nd century AD under Emperor Trajan, when it covered all of Europe and some of Africa and Asia. Beginning in the 3rd century AD, it began to collapse. The size of the empire made it hard to govern. But contentment, pride, self-sufficiency, sloth, and internal fighting were all internal attitudes that led to its fall. You might call these attitudes "spiritual drag."

The point I'm making is that from golf balls to empires, quick starts don't equal long-term sustainability. Internal and external "drag" slow them down. The same is true of our spiritual walk. We can start quickly, with plenty of enthusiasm, but internal and external drag can grind our spiritual progress to a halt. Solomon was influenced by both, and they led to catastrophe. The external drag was the allure of pagan women. God told Solomon not to intermarry with pagan women because they would lead his heart away from God and into idolatry. The internal drag was the pride, self-sufficiency, laziness, boredom, and apathy in his own heart. Solomon married 300 women and had 700 concubines to test the limits of human pleasure. As God warned, they led him into idolatry, and he then led Israel into idolatry and destruction.

When some of us first became Christians, we were flying fast, just like a golf ball off the face of a driver. We were learning so much. God seemed to answer our prayers immediately. We were reading our Bibles every day, soaking up everything we could about our new faith. Over time, we may have experienced drag in the form of the trials of life, unanswered prayer, or scorn and mocking from family or co-workers. We can also become victims of internal drag like Solomon and the Roman Empire. We tend to think that we have learned all that we need to, that we are spiritually mature, that since we've read the Bible several times, we don't need to read it anymore. In other words, we become victims of the drag of contentment, laziness, self-sufficiency, pride, and boredom.

I want us to be reminded of Luke 2:52: "And Jesus kept increasing in wisdom and stature, and in favor with God and men." Can you imagine that God Himself clothed in human flesh kept increasing in wisdom? How is that possible? When Jesus became a human being, He didn't stop being God. His humanity was added to His deity. In His humanity, He grew in wisdom and stature. He developed mentally and physically. He also devoted Himself to prayer.

If Jesus grew in wisdom, we should continue to do the same. Let's understand that God is not finished with us. We are not yet what God wants us to be. None of us should have the attitude that we are spiritually mature "enough". None of us should be satisfied with whatever progress we have made. We need self-examination and reflection. Have we unintentionally fallen victim to the silent killers of our spiritual growth? Are we spiritual "fat cats"? Do we think we have "arrived" spiritually? We need to resist spiritual drag. Satan can sniff it out and use it to cause our fall.

Pretend that today is New Years' Day. Set some goals and make some resolutions. Most of us resolve to lose weight and exercise on Jan 1. Those are great physical goals. Resolve to set some spiritual goals too. Make them realistic. Begin reading the Bible daily and journaling your thoughts and prayers as you go. Keep a journal of answered prayers. Serve somewhere. Memorize some of the well-known passages of scripture. Look for a mentor and for someone to mentor. Read the Bible all the way through in a year. Post notes around your house that remind you to pray and to thank God for His blessings. These are just some suggestions to help us resist the spiritual drag that will slow our walk with God. Start your new spiritual life today like you're a golf ball whizzing down the fairway!

REFLECTIONS:

- Christians should never stop growing spiritually. Discuss which of the above suggestions you can put into practice to guard against spiritual drag? Can you list some others?

- Do you still have the joy you had when you first believed in Jesus? If not, how can you get it back?

THE SCALE IS A CRUEL TASKMASTER

Romans 8:1: "There is therefore now no condemnation for those in Christ Jesus."

ONE OF MY ANNUAL NEW YEARS' RESOLUTIONS IS TO TRY to lose weight. According to a recent survey, it's the number one New Years' resolution for Americans. 21.4% of Americans resolved to do it. The next closest resolution on the list was life/self-improvements at 12.3%, followed by better financial decisions at 8.5%, and quitting smoking at 7.1%. These are all admirable goals. You may have heard that goals should be SMART: Specific, Measurable, Achievable, Relevant, and Time-Bound. Let me focus on the M, measurable. Weight loss is certainly that. We measure weight loss by stepping on a scale, but the scale is a cruel taskmaster.

It is cold, mechanical, insensitive, harsh, and exacting. I stand on mine every week with a mixture of hope and dread while it calculates. In that one second of waiting, my effort for the entire week will either be validated or voided. My scale blinks three times before rendering final judgment in menacing black digits against an icy blue background. The scale is merciless. It doesn't care how much I have exercised this week, or how many times I chose the salad over the cheesy burrito. It is heartless and without emotion. It tells the truth without regard for my feelings or how much its judgment may discourage me. It offers me no hope for the week to come. When I step on the scale for my weekly weigh-in, I know I will pay the price for every Ring Ding or M&M I may have eaten during the week, because the scale tells the truth without grace.

I wonder if you can tell where I'm going with this. In contrast to my severe scale is my gracious God. I believe that Jesus died for my sins and rose from the dead and because of that, I will be in heaven with Jesus one day. That's the good news of the gospel. The Bible says, "there is now no condemnation for those in Christ Jesus." Unlike my painstaking exertion to lose weight, my salvation does not depend on my effort, but on the work of Jesus who died for me. Unlike the cold and callous scale, my Savior loves me and gives me His abundant grace. He did *all* the work required for my salvation, dying to pay the penalty for my sin, taking the punishment that should be mine on Him. The Bible says of Jesus: "the Word became flesh, and dwelt among us, and we saw His glory, glory as of the only begotten from the Father, full of grace and truth." (John 1:14). When I stand before Jesus, I will not pay for any sin that I committed. The truth is that I deserve judgment, but because of His grace, I will receive mercy.

If you've ever tried to lose weight, you know that even when you haven't cheated the whole week, you still might not lose any weight. You might even have gained. You think you've done well that week, but on weigh-in day (judgment day), you find out that you have not. Maybe you ate something salty and you are retaining water. Maybe you didn't exercise as much as you thought. You can never be sure if you've done enough until you step on the scale. Thankfully, with Jesus, you never have to worry if you have done enough. He has done it all. All you need to do is believe.

The scale is a cruel taskmaster, but Jesus loves you more than you can ever know. Believe in Him today and know for certain that you have eternal life.

REFLECTIONS:

- What are some of the things people think they need to do to go to heaven?

- How does it make you feel that there is "no condemnation for those in Christ Jesus?"

- Consider the wrath that Jesus has saved you from and remember to praise Him this week!

GOD'S PERFECT JUSTICE

Psalm 9:8: "He will judge the world in righteousness. He will execute judgment for the peoples with equity."

I WAS SUMMONED FOR JURY DUTY IN JULY, 2019. ON Monday morning, I sat crammed in a room of over 500 prospective jurors. Eventually, my name was called as part of the jury pool for a criminal case. The jury pool was made up of 70 potential jurors from which the prosecution and defense select the 12 members of the jury. I was juror number 30 of 70. The defendant was charged with aggravated sexual assault on a child. I knew that because of the kind of case it was, many people would have legitimate concerns about serving. Because of that, I was reasonably sure that they would not fill the jury before they reached me at 30. I was not eager to serve either. I knew that if the lawyers questioned me that I could be assured that I would be excused by saying the magic words, "No I don't think I could judge this case fairly because a child is involved." Or I could have mentioned that I practiced law for twenty years. That usually does the trick. But I didn't do that. I felt obligated to be a fair and impartial juror. In my years of practicing law, that's all I would have asked from a prospective juror. Predictably, I was selected.

This was a very emotional case. The law required that we convict the defendant if we found beyond a reasonable doubt that he committed the offense with which he was charged. Otherwise, we had to acquit. After we heard the evidence and began our deliberations, I thought about our justice system. Our constitution guarantees the right to a jury trial, and that the defendant is presumed innocent until proven guilty. Put twelve strangers together in a room with various nationalities, cultures, religious backgrounds, and world-views and just about anything can happen. One very strong personality can dominate the room. Since criminal cases require a unanimous verdict to acquit or convict, one person can hang a jury and cause a mistrial. Jurors can hear the same evidence and come to opposite conclusions.

In our case, we were asked to determine a man's guilt or innocence of a crime that could put him in jail for many years. I've never held that power over someone else's life before. It's an incredible responsibility and burden to bear. We all wanted him to pay if he was guilty, and to protect the victim and others from him. People asked questions like, "Can I put a man away for that length of time on this evidence?" "Can I live with myself if it turns out he did this and I helped set him free?" "What if I believe he did *something*, but it doesn't rise to the level of the crime he's charged with?" "What does reasonable doubt mean anyway?"

We wrestled over the evidence. We grappled with our emotions. Eventually, we decided that he was guilty of inappropriate behavior, but there was not enough evidence to convict him of aggravated sexual assault on a child. So a man who is most definitely guilty of something is free today. My heart hurt. I had a pit in my stomach. I have a daughter. Many of you do too. I think about other people's daughters who could be this man's next victims. I prayed that he would receive help before there is another victim. I asked myself, "Did I do my duty?" I tried to uphold the rule of law as best as I could. That means I can't find him guilty of *this* crime just because he's probably guilty of *some* crime. It's not a perfect system. Sometimes, the innocent are convicted and the guilty go free. Trial by a jury of our peers is our American way. Though flawed, it's still the best system of justice that man has ever devised. It's the very best that humans can do.

I'm grateful that though our system is flawed, God's system of judgment has no flaws. God never has to wonder if He has all the facts, if someone is lying, if the video has been altered, if the statements were taken out of context, if the confession was coerced, or anything else. As the perfect, omniscient creator and judge of the universe, knowledge is not an issue for Him. He has perfect knowledge. Justice is not an issue for Him either. Psalm 7:11: "God is a righteous judge." Psalm 9:8: "He will judge the world in righteousness. He will execute judgment for the peoples with equity." Isaiah 11:4: "But with righteousness He will judge the poor, And decide with fairness for the afflicted of the earth; And He will strike the earth with the rod of His mouth, And with the breath of His lips He will slay the wicked."

As I beat myself up about whether we as a jury did the right thing, here's what I know. 1) If our jury set a guilty man free, God still has the power to judge, and He will judge perfectly. 2) I have to accept my limited knowledge and ability to administer justice. Only God's knowledge and judgment are perfect. God says, "Vengeance is mine. I will repay" (Deuteronomy 32:35 HCSB). 3) God is still sovereign. Maybe this man is free today because God has a different plan for his life than a long stretch of time in prison. Maybe God will use him to help other sex offenders. 4) Our God is a God of grace. During jury selection, we were asked if we believed that a sex offender can be rehabilitated, or do we believe "once a sex offender, always a sex offender." I thought, with the Holy Spirit, anyone can be rehabilitated. I was. God saved a wretch like me. If you're a believer, you were too. I pray that by the grace of God, this man will see the beauty of Jesus Christ and be saved and changed too. God is mighty to save.

REFLECTIONS:

- Discuss a time when you were wrongly accused of something. How did that make you feel?

- Recall a sin you committed, even if no one else knew about it. Journal your gratitude for God's mercy in pouring out His judgment on Jesus instead of you.

5

OUR NEW ROOMBA

Hebrews 2:14: "Because God's children are human beings—made of flesh and blood—the Son also became flesh and blood." (NLT)

A ROOMBA IS A ROBOT VACUUM CLEANER THAT VACUUMS your house for you. My wife has wanted one for some time. She's heard how great it is by word of mouth from her friends. As a sensitive and prudent husband of 25 years, I have learned that it's not good etiquette to buy cleaning machines or exercise equipment for your wife. As much as she may have wanted a Roomba, I thought it better not to commit the marital faux pas of buying a vacuum for her as a gift. Well, she got some gift cards for Christmas, waited for a sale, and with a 20% off coupon from Bed, Bath and Beyond, behold, we now own a Roomba! I have not seen my wife this happy since the birth of our children!

YOU CAN PROGRAM IT TO WORK IN CERTAIN AREAS FROM AN app on your phone. After it has finished vacuuming the defined area, it returns to its base to recharge its batteries. It's fresh and ready to go the next time you want to use it. When you wake up in the morning, your house is vacuumed. It comes in handy, especially when you have an ever-shedding dog. The beauty of it is that it does the work that we don't want to do without procrastinating, complaining, or demanding payment.

All of this got me thinking about the one thing that we all have to do, that none of us wants to do, and that is, to die. Wouldn't it be great if someone died for us so that we wouldn't have to die? We could just continue on blissfully because someone was kind enough to die in our place. Of course, someone *has* already died in our place. Jesus came down from heaven, leaving His place of glory as the second person of the Trinity, and became a man. He lived a sinless life and died on a cross to pay our sin debt to God. Then God the Father raised Him from the dead and exalted Him back to the place He occupied before He became a man. Everyone who trusts in His finished work on the cross for salvation will go to heaven. All because Jesus has done the work for us.

Now, if we are going to get excited about the work a Roomba can do, why would we not get excited about the work that Jesus did? When I come down in the morning, there is no dog hair on my kitchen floor. That's great, but honestly, it would take me less than five minutes of pushing a vacuum around to accomplish what the Roomba did while I was asleep. Jesus did work that I could not do if I had 1000 lifetimes. Only Jesus could pay the penalty for sin because only He is God, and only He became a man and lived a sinless life, which qualified Him to serve as our substitute. Because of Jesus' work, I receive something immeasurably better than a clean kitchen floor, I get eternal life!

I'm as guilty as anyone of trying to find ways to make my life easier. I love online banking, GPS navigation on my phone, and a host of other modern conveniences. But some things can't be fixed with technology. We experience health scares, money concerns, and relational tension. We worry about the daily difficulties of life, praying that God would make our lives easier, or praying that if God would just take care of this "one thing" for us, we could relax. The truth is that God *has* taken care of the one thing we need so that we can relax. Hebrews 2:14-15: "Because God's children are human beings—made of flesh and blood—the Son also became flesh and blood. For only as a human being could He die, and only by dying could He break the power of the devil, who had the power of death. Only in this way could he set free all who have lived their lives as slaves to the fear of dying" (NLT). We don't need to fear death because Jesus died for us. Death is a gateway to eternal life with Him.

My one complaint about the Roomba is that if you don't contain it to a smallish area, its battery will die before the work is done. When Jesus died on the cross, He said, "It is finished." That means He has done *all* the work necessary for our salvation. So enjoy your Roomba; enjoy other helpful technology. Making our lives easier is fine, but our primary goal is to be sure that we and others will make it to heaven. Remember that Jesus did greater work, which brought a greater benefit to us than anything else we could have on earth. He bought the one thing we could never buy: our souls!

REFLECTIONS:

- What is one modern convenience that makes your life easier and describe how?

- Eternity in heaven with Jesus will be amazing. How has faith in Jesus helped you in the past? How does it make your life better today?

6

TIME, THE MOST PRECIOUS COMMODITY

Psalm 118:24: "This is the day which the Lord has made; Let us rejoice and be glad in it."

THERE'S A PARK BENCH ON MY REGULAR RUNNING ROUTE with an index-card sized gold plaque inscribed with the name of a young man who died at 23 years old. Next to the plaque is a small plastic vial that holds a flower. I run that route at least three times a week. Every week for as long as I can remember, there has been a fresh red rose with baby's breath in that vase. I've never seen the person replace the dying rose with a new one, but it's obviously done by someone who loved him very deeply, and misses him more than seems bearable. I imagine a grieving mother or father, faithfully visiting that park bench every week, shedding many tears for their son who left this earth way too young.

When we lose a loved one, we want so much to honor their memory and to keep it alive. We don't know what else to do when we are grief-stricken, so we tend to our loved one's gravestone, or we place flowers in vases on a park bench. I think it makes us feel like we have some measure of control over a situation that we actually have no control over whatsoever. I'm not demeaning this at all. I would probably do the same if I was his parent.

Death is the great equalizer. It does not discriminate. Young or old, rich or poor, male or female, it simply doesn't matter. Unless Jesus returns first, every one of us will die. It's just a question of when. Some of us live for 90 or more years. Some of us don't even live a year. Our days are in God's hands. The value of a life is not measured in the quantity of years we live, but in the quality of those years. What we do with our time matters to God. Our days are a gift from Him. So how do we spend our most precious commodity?

1. We thank God for it. One of the most well-known verses in the Psalms is 118:24: "This is the day which the Lord has made; Let us rejoice and be glad in it." There are so many people who we meet who seem to be genuinely unhappy. We may even be among them. Even when enduring sadness or stress, we should always be able to find a reason to be thankful.

2. We do good with it. Ephesians 2:10: "For we are God's handiwork, created in Christ Jesus to do good works, which God prepared in advance for us to do." (NIV) God has already predetermined the work that He has for us to do. Let's not be cavalier about doing it. We all need to rest. But there's a difference between rest and sloth. God created the Sabbath for rest. But God cautions against laziness. Proverbs 6:10-11: " A little sleep, a little

slumber, a little folding of the hands to rest'—Your poverty will come in like a vagabond, and your need like an armed man" (NIV). God plans for us to use our time to provide for ourselves and our families. But He also wants us to do good to others. Galatians 6:10: "So then, while we have opportunity, let us do good to all people, and especially to those who are of the household of the faith."

3. We trust God with it. Psalm 31:14-15: "But as for me, I trust in You, O LORD. I say, "You are my God. My times are in Your hand." Most of us spend a lot of time worrying about our health. I do it too. That's why I'm out running in the first place! But our time is in God's hands. We will live as long as He wants us to and until we have accomplished what He has for us to do. Then He will bring us home.

I spent the first 35 years or so of my life as an unbeliever. I spent some of that time productively. I received an education, married an awesome woman, had two kids, and bought a house. But around those major events, I wasted so much time that it literally sickens me to think about it. Time is our most precious commodity. It can only be spent once. I'll never get that wasted time back. I think about that young man who lived only 23 years. I don't know what he did with his time. I don't know if he is in heaven. I don't know about his relationship with whoever is putting flowers in that vase every week. But I bet that they would give all they have for one more day with him. Spend each day productively. Don't take time for granted. You don't know how much you have. Give each day back to God as an offering to Him. There's no more rewarding feeling than knowing you have been productive for God's purposes and His glory. A life well-lived is a life lived for God.

REFLECTIONS:

- Take an inventory this week of how you spend your free time. We all need some down-time, but how could you spend your free time more productively?

- If Jesus told you that He was coming back tomorrow, what would you do with your last day?

7

THE PERIL OF TRUSTING YOUR EYES

Proverbs 14:12: "There is a way which seems right to a man, but its end is the way of death." (HCSB)

OUR CHURCH BUILDING HAS A LONG, NARROW CORRIDOR with windows from floor to ceiling on each side. You can see through this windowed corridor from one end of the church property to the other. It's neither good nor bad for people, but it's deadly for birds. One day I was in my office working on a sermon when I heard several thumps against the corridor window. I kept getting up to see if someone was knocking at the door. The last time I went out to look, I figured out what the sounds were. Pretty yellow-breasted birds were trying to fly through what appeared to them to be open space, but they had crashed hard into the glass and died.

Tragically, their eyes deceived them. These birds thought they were seeing open space to fly through, but what their eyes had perceived and their minds trusted resulted in death for them. It's not safe for us to trust our eyes either. We may trust our eyes and believe that what we see is good, but the result may either be a wrong decision, or worse, ensnarement into sin, or even death. Solomon wrote Proverbs 14:12: "There is a way which seems right to a man, but its end is the way of death."

But Solomon also provided solutions to the problem. The best way to avoid trusting our eyes is to trust in the Lord. The most well-known proverb is probably 3:5-6: "Trust in the Lord with all your heart, and do not lean on your own understanding. In all your ways acknowledge Him, and He will make your paths straight." Solomon also taught us to rely on the word of God. Proverbs 16:20: "He who gives attention to the *word* will find good, and blessed is he who trusts in the Lord." He also taught us to listen to the wisdom of others. He wrote in Proverbs 12:15: "The way of a fool is right in his own eyes, but a wise man is he who listens to counsel."

To avoid the destruction that can result from trusting our own eyes, we can trust in the Lord, rely on His word, and seek the counsel of others. Why then do we continue to make bad decisions or fall into the same patterns of sin? I think it's because we are wise in our own eyes. That's the sin of pride, and it leads to all kinds of negative consequences. When we refuse to ask God for direction in our lives and choose to go it alone, and when we ignore His Word, we can be sure that we will soon find ourselves outside of God's will. When we live our lives in isolation from the counsel of other believers who can speak truth and wisdom into our lives, we are spurning the very people whom God has placed in our lives to help us.

Simply put, if we want to be fruitful Christians, we must be humble enough to admit that we cannot be wise until we seek wisdom. We don't have innate wisdom. That's why Solomon taught his son to seek wisdom more than anything else. He said it was more profitable than silver or gold. Wisdom comes from the Holy Spirit, the Bible, and other believers.

This has several applications. The most important thing is to spend time alone with Jesus in prayer. We all say we want to do this, but often we don't make the time. I've never met anyone who said that they were completely satisfied with their prayer life. We don't want to approach this legalistically, where we require ourselves to get up at 5 a.m. every morning and spend at least an hour in prayer and Bible study. We will most likely be setting ourselves up for failure and the guilt that goes with it. But we do want to make a concerted effort to have a time and a place where we can be intentional with our relationship with God. All relationships require an investment of time. Our relationship with Jesus is no different.

A second thing we can do is to be sure that we have at least one or two close friends who we can trust to speak truth into our lives. Developing these relationships takes time. When we wade into the shallow water with them and they haven't hurt us, we can risk going a little deeper as they do the same with us. That's how strong relationships are built. If you've been hurt before by trusting someone, I hope that you'll try again.

As I heard these loud thuds against the windows, I wished that just one of these birds could gain wisdom, go back to the nest, and tell the rest not to go that way. Sadly, there was nothing I could do at the time to help. How can you communicate with birds? But God has communicated with us. He has given us resources so that we will not walk the path that leads to destruction, but will live a fruitful life. Let's take advantage of the gifts God has provided.

P.S. We've since installed colored tape on the windows and the problem has been solved to the delight of the birds!

REFLECTIONS:

- Discuss a time when you made a poor decision without praying and seeking wisdom from others.

- How might that situation have turned out differently if you prayed and sought the advice of a wise friend first?

- Give an example of when you prayed and sought advice and it resulted in a better decision.

8

HAVE A HAPPY HEART

John 5:6: "Do you want to be made well?" (NRSV)

"Do you want to be made well?" This was the question Jesus asked the paralytic in John 5. We've all known people who are difficult to be around because they are always complaining about their health, their finances, their job, their family, or many other things. They seem to carry around this cloud of negativity that you can almost visibly see, like Pigpen's cloud of filth in the Charlie Brown cartoon. I watched Winnie the Pooh as a kid. Whenever Winnie, Tigger, Piglet, or any of the other characters met Eeyore, the sad-sack donkey, they would always find him complaining. He was always pessimistic and depressed. Some people live their lives expecting bad things to happen.

The human experience is difficult. We do suffer physical and emotional pain. We are under ever-increasing stress and anxiety in the fast-paced, communication and information age, where everyone has immediate access to us. I love my Iphone, but there are times when I would like to throw it in a lake just to have some peace. But then I'd be anxious knowing that I'd be missing emails, texts, and phone calls! How we respond to the pressures of life says a lot about our walk with Christ. We can be complainers or we can be thanksgivers. (I think I just made up a word.)

Moses led the Israelites out of Egypt, out of bondage, and into the desert. That should have been a time of great thanksgiving and celebration for the Israelites. God freed them after 400 years of slavery. But as soon as they left Egypt, they started complaining. "Where will we find food to eat?" "What shall we drink?" "Are there no graves in Egypt that you brought us out into the wilderness to die?" The Israelites lacked a heart of gratitude. It seemed like they found joy in complaining. If we are going to make the most of the life that God has given us, we have to have an attitude of thanksgiving. There will always be things that we would like to change. We wish this ache or pain would go away. We long for a better relationship with family. The list goes on and on. Complaining can become a way of life. Before we know it, our complaints become part of our identity. We turn them into excuses for not living life to the fullest. We allow ourselves to take on the mindset of a victim, always seeking sympathy from others for our sorry lot in life. We can't enjoy life with that attitude.

When Jesus asked the man at the pool of Bethesda, "Do you want to be made well?", he responded, "Sir, I have no man to put me into the pool when the water is stirred up,

but while I am coming, another steps down before me"
(HCSB). He made excuses for his sad condition, which he
had been in for 38 years! You expect his answer to be,
"YES I want to be made well!" Instead, his paralysis was
part of who he was. He depended on it to beg alms from
passersby, and I'm not sure he *did* want to be made
well. Jesus healed him anyway.

I recently read Corrie ten Boom's classic book, *The
Hiding Place*. Corrie and her sister Betsie had been sent to
a new concentration camp in Ravensbruck, Germany, and
forced to live in cramped and disgusting quarters. They
shared a bed with 3-4 other women and the entire
barracks was flea-infested; so much so that the guards
would not even enter the building. They sure had reason
to complain, but Corrie and Betsie rejoiced that the
guards would not enter. They took hold of 1 Thess. 5:18,
"In everything give thanks, for this is God's will for you in
Christ Jesus," and made it their verse for the place. They
gave thanks that they had been assigned to live together
and that they had a copy of the Bible that the guards
wouldn't find since they wouldn't enter. They rejoiced
that since they were packed so tightly together, other
women would hear them read from it. They thanked God,
even for the fleas that allowed them to share the
gospel. Tragically, Betsie died in that camp, but she died
with a thankful heart. Corrie survived and shared the
gospel internationally for decades.

We have a choice. We can grumble or give thanks in all
circumstances. Let's make it our goal to give thanks no
matter what we face. God can provide water from rocks,
manna from the sky, and fleas to drive out guards, so the

Word can be studied and proclaimed, even in a concentration camp defined by death. Complaining doesn't change anything. But God can turn any circumstance into an opportunity for someone with a grateful heart.

REFLECTIONS:

- Why is it draining to spend with complainers?

- Our attitude can make a big difference in every situation. Would those closest to you say you are more an Eyeore or a Tigger? Why?

- Discuss a time when God worked things out for good through a difficult circumstance and what you learned.

9

ULTIMA THULE AND ULTIMATE VALUE

Ecclesiastes 3:11: "He has also set eternity in the human heart." (NIV)

SINCE THE INVENTION OF THE REMOTE CONTROL, WE NO longer have to get up to change channels. (Kids, ask your parents!) Remember the old lady who was on the television commercials selling "the Clapper"? She showed us that we don't have to get up to turn off the lights. Pizza delivery means dinner dropped off at our door. We may barely be willing to move to perform menial tasks, but humans will spare no expense or effort to explore something new.

Scientists recently directed New Horizons, a spacecraft that photographed Pluto and its moons, on a flyby of a space rock called "Ultima Thule." Pluto is about 3.1 billion miles from earth. Ultima Thule is another billion miles away! It took 13 years for New Horizons to reach Ultima Thule at 36,400 mph, at an approximate cost of $700 million. Ultima Thule is just a big, brownish-gray, snowman-shaped rock, about 19 miles long and 12 miles across.

What is it about space that is so compelling that we will expend this amount of money and effort to see pictures of a giant rock? I think it's the longing of the human heart and mind to know that there is something else out there. We want to know that we are not alone, that somehow, we are joined to something else in this unfathomably vast universe. I also think that the human heart was made for adventure. We were made to explore. Magellan, Columbus, Cortes, Ponce de Leon, Pizarro, Lewis & Clark, and many others dedicated their lives to exploration. We are always trying to fill our empty hearts with something outside of ourselves, whether in our world or beyond it. We can be like the Greeks in ancient Athens, who "used to spend their time in nothing other than telling or hearing something new." (Acts 17:21).

I love space exploration. I am fascinated by a snowman-shaped rock 4.1 billion miles away. If it were on earth, most people wouldn't look at it twice, but put it 4.1 billion miles away, and now it's a fascination that captures our imagination. But if we think that we will find any ultimate satisfaction in anything found in our solar system or beyond it, we will be disappointed. Reaching Ultima Thule only makes astronomers ask, "What's next?" Astronomers have recently discovered another body in our solar system called "Farout", which lies 120 Astronomical Units, or AU, from the sun. (One AU is 93 million miles, the distance from the earth to the sun.) By comparison, Ultima Thule is about 40 AU from earth. What if we ever reach Farout? Well, soon after Farout was discovered, scientists found a new body called "Farfarout," which is 140 AU from earth. What if we reach Farfarout? Will we ever be satisfied?

We won't because the quest for anything other than God will only leave us with a hunger for more. Seventeenth-century French philosopher and scientist Blaise Pascal said, "Our hearts have a 'God-shaped hole' in them that only God can fill." Ecclesiastes 3:11 says "He has also set eternity in the human heart." The entire book of Ecclesiastes is Solomon's testimony about how he tried to gain satisfaction in everything under the sun: food, women, knowledge, pleasure, building projects, labor, and it was all meaningless. There was no ultimate value in any of it. Nothing satisfied him other than God. That's because there is nothing of ultimate value apart from God. Jesus is the only One who can ultimately satisfy our anxious longings and fill our empty hearts. He helps us through life and brings us safely to heaven when our lives are over. If you have a hole in your heart that you can't seem to fill, that's because the hole in your heart is God-shaped. No amount of food, drink, money, pleasure, sex, travel, or anything else will ever fill it. Only God can fill the longing of the human heart for eternity with His Son Jesus.

Reflections:

- What are some things that you rely on to satisfy you other than God?

- Describe a specific time when you were looking for satisfaction from the things of the world, and what was the result?

- Recount a time when you realized that God was all you needed.

THE NEED FOR CREDIT

John 5:44: "How can you believe, when you receive glory from one another and you do not seek the glory that is from the one and only God?"

I HAVE A FITBIT WATCH THAT TRACKS THE NUMBER OF STEPS I walk each day. My daily goal is 8000 steps. When I reach it, my watch starts buzzing. Rockets and fireworks flash on the screen, congratulating me for my accomplishment. I also recently bought a used exercise bike from someone in my neighborhood. I love it because I can still get my exercise when I don't feel like braving cold-winter mornings. The problem with the bike is that I can pedal as hard as I can to the end of my endurance, and I won't get credit on my Fitbit for a single step because my arms aren't moving. That's not a workable system for me. If I do the work, I want the credit. I want my watch to buzz furiously. I *need* to see the rockets and fireworks to validate my achievement. If it's 10 p.m. and I'm 500 steps short, I'll do laps around my kitchen and living room until I get that credit.

Why is it that we seek validation and approval? Why is it so important to us that we get the credit we think we deserve? Why do I need my watch to congratulate and affirm me?! Isn't that crazy?! There are many ways that our need for approval, validation, and credit shows itself. We may get ourselves in debt trying to buy things that will impress others. Someone said, "We spend money we don't have, on things we don't need, to impress people we don't like." We may get ourselves into trouble at work by trying to take more credit for a project than we deserve, or belittling someone else's work to elevate our own. We become unbearable to others when we constantly boast of our accomplishments.

Living for the approval and validation of others was a problem in Jesus' day too. He said in John 5:44, "How can you believe, when you receive glory from one another and you do not seek the glory that is from the one and only God?" Their priorities were skewed. Jesus was talking to the religious leaders who liked to walk around in long robes and pray long public prayers so that the people would heap praise on them for their piety. Jesus told them not to seek the praise of others, but to seek the glory of God. We aren't any different. When we give, we want people to know about it. When we visit the sick or do some other good deed, we want credit.

Cheerios recently ran an ad campaign with Ellen DeGeneres called, "Thanks for all the good you do." If you reported the good work you did on a postcard from the back of the Cheerios box, you could win tickets to Ellen's show. It was an effective campaign because it motivated people to help others, but we are not to do benevolent deeds for earthly reward. Matthew 6:3-4 says, "When you give to the poor, do not let your left hand know what your right hand is doing, so that your giving will be in secret; and your Father who sees what is done *in secret* will reward you."

That's the crux of the matter. Do we want honor from men or from God? There's nothing wrong and everything right with helping others. That's what we should be doing. The issue is our motivation. If we are doing these deeds for earthly credit, then as Jesus said, we already have our reward in full. But if we are doing these deeds so that men may see our good works and glorify God, then we are doing them for the right reasons.

So how do we change our hearts so that we don't need the credit for the good that we do, and are satisfied that God receives all the glory? Harry Truman is credited with saying, "It's amazing what you can accomplish if you don't care who gets the credit." Not caring if we get credit requires a humble heart, recognizing that our financial surplus that allows us to give, or our health that allows us to run errands for someone in need, or any knowledge we have to teach others, are all gifts from God. Paul said, "If you received it from God, why do you boast as if you did not?" We need to humble our hearts and seek the approval of One. People are fickle. You'll constantly need to gain their approval again. Affirmation can become addicting and toxic. If God knows what you've done, let that be enough. Pray about where you are having problems in this area and ask God to change your heart.

REFLECTIONS:

- Do you consider yourself to be more of a God-pleaser or a people-pleaser? Why?

- What are some of the ways that you seek the approval of people rather than the approval of God?

- How can you test yourself to ensure that you want God's approval more than the approval of people?

11

CONFLICTED OVER CONFLICT

Exodus 3:12: "Certainly I will be with you."

IF YOU'RE LIKE ME, YOU DON'T NECESSARILY THRIVE ON conflict. Conflict sells on television and in the movies. We invest ourselves in the characters to see how the tension resolves. At the end, the conflicts are resolved, the loose ends are tied up, and we can either turn off the TV or leave the movie theater and go home. In real life, conflict is not always resolved in a neat 2-hour window. Usually conflict lasts much longer, is harder to fix, more painful, and causes us worry and sleepless nights. Conflict is a part of life. Avoiding it most often only makes it worse. Like pressure and stress, the only way to survive conflict is to learn how to diffuse it.

There is plenty of conflict in the Bible. When God called Moses to go tell Pharaoh to let the Israelites go, Moses did everything he could to avoid that assignment. He claimed that he was not eloquent but slow of speech. He argued that they wouldn't believe that God had sent him. He pleaded for God to give a sign confirming that He had sent him. After God answered all of Moses' protests, all out of objections, Moses simply begged God to send someone else. Moses knew that he would have to confront his past in Egypt. He would also have to bump heads with the most powerful man in the world to free the Israelites from captivity. He was terrified. Pharaoh could easily kill him or make him a slave. Moses asked God, "Who am I that I should go to Pharaoh and that I should bring the sons of Israel out of Egypt." God's answer to Moses in Exodus 3:12 is *the* answer to resolving all conflict. God told Moses, "Certainly I will be with you."

The answer to how we handle conflict is so simple, though not easy. We may not have the strength in ourselves to handle the conflict. We may be outnumbered and overmatched, but God promises to send His incredible power with us. God said, "I will be with you." In Moses' case, we know how the story ended. God sent ten plagues on Egypt until Pharaoh finally let the Israelites go. Then Pharaoh changed his mind and pursued them as far as the Red Sea to either kill them or capture them and return them to Egypt. The Egyptians pinned Moses and the Israelites against the Red Sea. It seemed like curtains for them. Then God parted the Red Sea by the hand of Moses and the Israelites escaped on dry land. When the Egyptians tried to cross, the sea covered them. God proved Himself faithful and true to Moses. He was with Moses.

Is Moses' story relevant to you and me? When Jesus was about to be taken up to heaven, the last thing He said to the apostles was this: "Go therefore and make disciples, baptizing them in the name of the Father, Son and Holy Spirit, and teaching them to obey all that I commanded you and lo, *I will be with you always,* even to the end of the age" (Matt. 28:19-20). Before He left His disciples, He promised to send to them the Holy Spirit, who would never leave them (John 14:16). Most conflict is the result of disagreement with our boss, spouse, child, parent, or friend. It comes in forms too numerous to count. Does Jesus' promise matter in those conflicts? I believe that it does. Think about how Jesus lived. His life was filled with conflict with the religious leaders of Israel. Jesus was never flustered. He asked questions. He told stories. He helped people understand His point of view even if they refused to agree with it.

Whenever you are about to enter into a conflict, pray. Remind Jesus of His promise to be with you. His Holy Spirit will give you the words to speak. Listen to the other person, but listen to the voice of the Holy Spirit too. Don't speak until you're sure that you understand your opponent, and have heard from the Holy Spirit. Learn from Jesus. Listen. Ask questions. Tell stories. Trust His promises. I'm a long way from having these principles mastered. That said, I can recount several times that I have experienced peace by resolving conflict while relying on the Holy Spirit's wisdom, and fistfights when I have relied on my own. Seriously. Conflict resolution is a whole lot easier when we rely on His divine wisdom. Sometimes, God won't let us go around conflict, but He has promised to be with us in it, and to see us through it.

REFLECTIONS:

- Recall a memory of when you went out of your way to avoid conflict and how it worked out.

- Describe a time when you trusted God to help you through a conflict and how it was resolved.

- Write down steps that you will take to manage conflict the next time it arises?

12

OVERCOMING DISAPPOINTMENT

Job 2:10: "Should we accept only good things from the hand of God and never anything bad?"

IN JANUARY 2018, SOME KID THAT PRACTICALLY NOBODY had ever heard of named Tua Tagovailoa came off the bench for Alabama's football team to start the second half of the national championship game against Georgia. He made big play after big play, leading Alabama to an epic comeback. In overtime, he threw a perfect pass that resulted in the game-winning, and national championship-winning touchdown. After the game, Tua praised his coaches, his teammates and most importantly, the Lord Jesus Christ. He was very vocal about his faith. The next year, he became an even bigger star. He finished second in the voting for the Heisman Trophy. He led his team to a 14-0 record, and Alabama was favored to repeat as the national champion, this time against Clemson.

. . .

THINGS DIDN'T GO AS TUA AND THE TIDE HOPED IN THE title game. Clemson dominated in every aspect and won convincingly, 44-16. In this game, a new star was born, Trevor Lawrence, a freshman quarterback sensation from Cartersville High School in Georgia. Before the game, Lawrence was asked how he keeps his composure in the big moments. He said, "Football's important to me, but it's not my life. It's not the biggest thing in my life. I would say my faith is. That just comes from knowing who I am outside of that. No matter how big the situation is, it's not going to define me. I put my identity in what Christ says, who He thinks I am and who I know that He says I am." Meanwhile, his coach, Dabo Swinney, could not stop praising God and giving God the glory after the game on national television! I don't know what's going on in college football, but I like it!

Back to Tua. His teammates told him after the game that his life would not be defined by this loss. He knew that was true, and he planned to be back at Alabama for the 2020 season to chase another national championship. After the Clemson game, Tua said that Alabama was good, but, "Good is not good enough." He was crushed by the defeat and took it hard. That led me to think, what is the biblical response to disappointment?

Job was a rich man, prospering in every way. But unbeknownst to him, he was the object of a cosmic contest between God and Satan. Satan said that Job only loved God because God had allowed him to prosper. But take away his prosperity, Satan argued, and he would curse God. God allowed Satan to take everything from Job: his children, servants, wealth and livestock, and finally his health. The only thing he left him with was his wife. He probably wished she was the one thing God had taken! After he had lost so much, she said to him, "Do you still hold your integrity? Curse God and die!" Not exactly an encouraging word! Job answered, "Should we accept only good things from the hand of God and never anything bad?" (Job 2:10 NLT)

That's the biblical perspective on how to handle life's disappointments. Job could have cursed God. He could have refused to accept the bad from God. He could have only loved God in times of prosperity and not in times of disappointment, or even incomprehensible loss. In the middle 38 chapters of the book, Job certainly had some questions for God, but he never cursed God. I find comfort in these verses because life is never without trouble for very long. Like Job, I want answers from God when disappointments seem to pile up and success and encouragement are rare. We would love our lives to look like a graph with time on the horizontal matrix and prosperity on the vertical matrix, and for the plotted line across time and prosperity to ascend in a straight line. But life isn't like that. Prosperity is mixed with adversity. Success is replaced by disappointment, and then vice-versa. Tua came back for the 2020 season, but got injured and had to sit out the remainder of the year. Great disappointment! But then he was drafted 5th overall to the Miami Dolphins. Great success!

Disappointment will only defeat us if we allow it. Often disappointment is a tool that God uses to achieve some greater purpose for our lives. Abraham, Isaac, Jacob, Joseph, Moses, David, Solomon, Peter, and many others experienced disappointment. God still used each of them. Thomas Edison had an idea, to invent an electric light bulb. He failed 100 times. When asked if he was disappointed, he said "Disappointed?! No! I've figured out 100 ways not to invent the light bulb!" Of course, he then successfully invented the light bulb and changed the world. If you're like me, you might feel like you've had enough disappointment for a lifetime already. But we should accept disappointment from God as instruction, try to learn God's lessons, and strive toward future success. God uses disappointment not to stunt our growth, but to launch it.

REFLECTIONS:

- Describe a time when you were greatly disappointed by something that God allowed.

- Share a time when God's answer to your prayer was even better than what you asked?

- Write how this might shape the way you handle disappointment in the future.

13

NO RETURNS, NO EXCHANGES

James 1:17: "Every good thing given and every perfect gift is from above."

DECEMBER 26 IS ONE OF THE BUSIEST DAYS OF THE RETAIL year. Most people who work in retail surprisingly say that the day after Christmas is worse than Christmas Eve. That's because December 26 is return and exchange day. All the people who were unsatisfied with their gifts return them to get what they really wanted, only without whatever Christmas spirit they may have had the day before. We all have people on our Christmas shopping list who are hard to buy for. It may not be that we are bad gift-givers. Some people are just tough. We always include the gift receipt for those people.

There is only One perfect gift giver; only One who knows exactly what we need, and that's God. James 1:17 says, "Every good thing given and every perfect gift is from above, coming down from the Father of lights, with whom there is no variation or shifting shadow." God knows everything we *need* and He graciously provides it. He doesn't always give us everything we want though. What are the things we need? We need a savior to save us from our sin. We need air to breathe, food to eat, and water to drink. God provides all of these. The things we want are new cars, houses, jobs, clothes, and other material things. None of these are bad, but most times they are not needs

I have never worked in retail. I just don't have the patience for it. If you go to just about any store the week after Christmas, from Macy's to Walmart, you will see a long line of people impatiently waiting to make their exchange or return. I feel so badly for people who work in customer service who have to listen to the never-ending complaints of angry shoppers. I would like to work on the return/exchange line in heaven. There would never be a single person on it. No one would ever be unhappy with the gift that God had given them. How could anyone be unhappy with the gift of Jesus Christ and the eternal life that belief in Him provides?

Our problem is that we are so focused on the material things of life, the temporal things of life, the things that don't last, and the things that have no eternal value, that we often don't spend any time focusing on the things that have eternal value. Paul put it like this: "Whatever is true, whatever is honorable, whatever is pure, whatever is lovely, whatever is of good repute, if there is any excellence and if anything is worthy of praise, dwell on these things. The things you have learned and received and heard and seen in me, practice these things and the God of peace will be with you all" (Phil. 4:8-9).

Paul wanted his readers to dwell on things of eternal significance, not the things of the world that are passing away. If we dwell on things we did not get for Christmas, we might be disappointed. Maybe there was something we desperately wanted, but I doubt if it was something we really needed. God has already given us everything we need. Whatever material gifts we receive from others are gravy, mere tokens of that person's love for us that will provide us with some temporary pleasure. When I think about the money we spent on our kids on Christmases long past; toys, video games, board games, clothes, and whatever else; the one thing all those gifts have in common is that we no longer have them! They are all in a landfill somewhere now! The only gift that lasts eternally is the gift of Jesus Christ and the benefits He brings.

If you are a believer in Jesus Christ, remember that you already have everything you will ever need. If you're not a believer, whatever you don't get for Christmas won't make you happy anyway. True happiness is only found in knowing Jesus Christ as Lord and Savior. That's the best gift ever. If you have that, you'll never want a refund, return, or exchange.

REFLECTIONS:

- What is the best Christmas gift you ever received? Do you still have it?

- Take time this week to look around at all of your stuff. Knowing that "you can't take it with you," how can you learn to value your eternity more than things that are only temporary?

- Has God ever ripped a material possession from your clinging hand? What did you learn from losing it?

14

EARNED TRUST

Psalm 9:10: "And those who know Your name will put their trust in You, For You, O Lord, have not forsaken those who seek You."

A COUPLE OF YEARS AGO, DOCTORS DIAGNOSED MY WIFE Molly with breast cancer. She had to undergo a variety of tests to see if her cancer had spread. They had to inject dye and allow it to course throughout her body. Before they could do that, they first had to be sure that she wasn't pregnant! Now that would be something! Let's just say that absent divine intervention, pregnancy was not possible.

Even though I knew she wasn't pregnant, I tried to imagine what it would be like to have her tell me that she was. First, she'd have to pick me up off the floor. Next, she would probably expect that I would be suspicious, so she would assure me that she has been faithful and that the baby is mine. Even though I would not understand how she could be pregnant, knowing Molly as I do, I would immediately accept that the miraculous had happened, rather than believe that she had been unfaithful. Over the 35+ years that I have known her, she has always been honest, loyal, truthful, dependable, and faithful. She's never given me any reason to suspect her of anything else.

As I thought about that, I considered the trustworthiness and faithfulness of our great God. There is so much in the Bible that is hard to understand. How could Sarah become pregnant at 90 years old? How could God part the Red Sea so the Israelites could cross? How could a donkey rebuke a man? How can a child be born of a virgin? I could go on and on. What about the things that happen to us that are hard to understand: Why does God allow evil? Why do bad things happen to good people? Why do the wicked prosper while the righteous suffer? What does God want me to learn from this difficult trial and when will it end? There are so many things about God that we just can't comprehend. Our temptation is to question God. How can God be good and tolerate evil? If God is really involved in His creation and in my life, He would remove this suffering from me.

This is dangerous thinking. It's how Satan twists the truth so we will believe a lie. Just like he did in the garden of Eden when he said to Eve in Gen. 3:2, "Indeed has God said, 'You shall not eat from any tree in the garden?'" From that simple, cunning question, Eve doubted God and ate the forbidden fruit. Eve lost sight of God's goodness and trustworthiness. God has proven that He is faithful and trustworthy to us over and over again. We know that He loves us because of Christmas, when

God became a man. We know that He loves us because of Good Friday, when Jesus died for our sins. We know that He loves us because of His Providence in our lives. How many times in your life has God worked out an impossible situation? How many times have circumstances "coincidentally" worked out for your good? That's God's Providence.

In any relationship, trust has to be earned. A reputation for honesty is a good start, but trust is earned by repeated minute by minute, hour by hour, day by day, year by year trustworthiness. There is no substitute for that. Molly has exhibited those characteristics as long as I have known her. God has too! David and others repeatedly wrote some form of "Trust God!" in the psalms. One of my favorites is Psalm 9:10: "And those who know Your name will put their trust in You, For You, O Lord, have not forsaken those who seek You."

Psalm 20:7: "Some trust in chariots and some in horses, but we trust in the name of the Lord our God." Every Christmas, we consider that for the season is the birth of our Savior. We remember also that He was born to die for our sins. How else could God earn our trust more than by becoming human and dying on the cross for us? God loves us. When our time on earth is done, He will deliver us home to His arms. He has promised us that, and our God has proven to be trustworthy.

REFLECTIONS:

- How have the people you trust the most proved their trustworthiness to you over the years?

- If someone hurt you, what would it take to regain your trust?

- God wants us to trust Him. Write down the ways that God has proved His trustworthiness to you.

15

GOLF HOLES AND BLACK HOLES

1 Corinthians 2:9: "Things which eye has not seen and ear has not heard, and which have not entered the heart of man, all that God has prepared for those who love Him."

MOST OF US HAVE A "BUCKET LIST", A LIST OF THINGS WE'D like to do or see before we "kick the bucket." In April 2019, I checked a big one off of my list. I went to Augusta National Golf Club to watch The Masters golf tournament. My first memory of watching the Masters was in 1986 when 46-year-old Jack Nicklaus shocked and delighted the golf world with a stunning come from behind win. I've watched the Masters every year since and have always wanted to walk those hallowed grounds. The golf course is even more spectacular in person than it is on TV. Every magnolia tree, every azalea bush, every blade of grass is perfectly manicured for this event. For a golf fan, it's a glimpse of heaven on earth, an absolute must see.

As incredible as that sight was, on the same day that I visited Augusta, astronomers identified and photographed a black hole. The picture showed a circle of bright light with darkness in the center. It's known as M87 and its mass (the measure of how much matter an object contains) is equal to 6.5 billion of our suns. A black hole is born when a large star explodes, creating a massive amount of gravity that devours everything that comes near it. Light and matter become brighter as they swirl around the "event horizon," the point of no return for the light and matter before the black hole swallows it. Can you imagine being able to get close enough to a black hole to watch that happen? That would put walking around a golf course to shame!

Now imagine this: Astronomers think that our own Milky Way galaxy may contain up to one billion black holes. That's in addition to the 100 billion stars in our galaxy. Now to completely blow your mind, astronomers say that the observable universe contains somewhere between 200 billion and 2 trillion galaxies! The human mind is unable to comprehend numbers of this size. My wife Molly and I share a love of travel. Seeing any new part of the earth for the first time is amazing. There's so much to see and not enough time. We want to visit Hawaii, the great northwest, Italy, Greece, Iceland, you name it, we want to go there. The earth is spectacular. There's no way we can see it all before we die. If the earth is spectacular, what about the rest of the universe? I love it when astronomers release pictures like M87. It's as close as I will ever get to space travel. At least in my present body.

The Bible says all believers will receive glorified bodies. We may be capable of seeing the entire universe from heaven. Or we may not even care about it because we will be in the presence of God who made the universe! If the universe is spectacular, can you even begin to imagine what heaven will be like? And if you can't imagine what heaven will be like, can you imagine gazing at God Himself?! 1 Corinthians 2:9: "Things which eye has not seen and ear has not heard, and which have not entered the heart of man, all that God has prepared for those who love Him." Think about that verse. Our eyes have seen some incredible, even inexplicable things in the universe. Our eyes have seen objects in the heavens of unimaginable size and beauty. Now our eyes have even seen black holes.

Yet the Bible says that God has prepared things for us that NO eye has seen, or ear heard, or even contemplated by the mind. Such is the glory of God and heaven that awaits. The Bible describes heaven as a city of pure gold, with foundations made from every precious stone on earth. There will be no sun or moon because God is the source of light. As amazing as that may be, even more so is that there will be no sin there. Only Jesus and those who bring Him glory will be there. Night and day we will worship Him. We will gaze upon His face.

When you think about the ultimate eradication of sin, sadness, tears, and death, that truly is more incredible than anything we have ever seen. What it will be like is beyond our imagination. It's more glorious than the universe and everything in it. We should examine ourselves to be sure that we will enter it at all costs. Have you accepted Jesus as your Lord and Savior and received His forgiveness for your sins? If you haven't, what are you waiting for? If you have, heaven awaits.

In the meantime though, if you ever get a chance to visit Augusta National, I have to say, it's not a bad place to wait!

REFLECTIONS:

- Take time to consider the size of the universe and how powerful God must be to have created it. Write a letter of thanks to God the Creator.

- Read 1 Cor. 2:9 and Psalm 8:3-4. Spend some time this week considering that the same God who created the universe loves you.

16

THE SHIFTING SAND OF FALSE EXPECTATION

John 16:33: "In this world you will have trouble, but take heart, I have overcome the world."

I WAS DRIVING PAST THE LOCAL RACE TRAC WHERE I usually buy gas and noticed that the price of gas was $1.79. I needed gas but there was no way I was going to pay $1.79 when I had just paid only $1.55 at the new Walmart the week before. Just a few months ago, when the price of gas was much higher, I would have felt like I was stealing if I bought gas for $1.79. But gas prices had dropped, and my expectations changed.

If you have ever been in the service business and had to tell someone how long the wait will be, you know it's better to estimate on the high side so they will be happy that they waited less time than the estimate you gave. Under-promise, over-deliver. It's all about creating proper expectations. People will always be disappointed when they get less than they expected.

The same is true of our expectations from God. If we believe the prosperity gospel preachers who teach that God wants us to be healthy and wealthy all the time, we will have no way to understand our suffering. If God is sovereign, the thinking goes, and He wants me to be healthy and wealthy, then how could I ever have to suffer? The problem is false expectations. The Bible is clear that we *will* suffer. Jesus said, "In this world you will have trouble" (John 16:33). The psalms are filled with laments from David and others written while suffering. Joseph was wrongfully thrown in jail. Daniel was exiled, betrayed, and nearly executed. According to tradition, Isaiah was sawn in two. Most of the other prophets suffered. All of the apostles except John were martyred. Jesus suffered more than anyone who ever lived. Why should we think we would be any different?

The good news is that if we have learned to expect to suffer sometimes, we won't be discouraged when it happens. Jesus also said, "but take courage, I have overcome the world." Jesus also said, "In My Father's house are many dwelling places; if it were not so, I would have told you; for I go to prepare a place for you. If I go and prepare a place for you, I will come again and receive you to Myself, that where I am, there you may be also" (John 14:2-3). Jesus' word is truth, so we should expect to suffer. We should also expect that Jesus will be with us in our suffering, and ultimately that when our time on earth is done, that we will spend eternity with Him. When we suffer, we should not ask, Why me? We should ask, why not me? Then we walk by faith asking the Lord to be with us and to help us through this challenging time.

The problem with expectations is that they constantly change. My level of satisfaction or disappointment with the price of gas depends on what I expect to pay, which is a moving target. It depends on economic factors that I can't control or understand. My level of satisfaction or disappointment with Jesus depends on my expectations of Him too. But unlike the price of gas, Jesus is not a moving target. Hebrews 13:8: "Jesus Christ is the same yesterday today and forever," so I know what to expect.

With the assurance of Jesus as my Savior, His promise that He will never leave me or forsake me, and that He has prepared a place for me, I can trust Him when I suffer. I pray that I will recognize His purpose in it and that He will use it for good. On Christ the solid rock I stand. All other ground, including the factors that affect the price of gas, is sinking sand.

REFLECTIONS:

- How would you explain John 16:33: "In this world you will have trouble, but take heart, I have overcome the world," to a 5th grader?

- Describe a time when God took you through trouble rather than allowing you to go around it. What did you learn?

- Which is harder for you, knowing that you will have trouble, or taking heart that He has overcome the world? How can you learn to take heart knowing that Jesus has overcome the world?

17

WHAT HAVE YOU DONE FOR ME LATELY?

John 6:26: "Truly, truly, I say to you, you seek Me, not because you saw signs, but because you ate of the loaves and were filled."

THE PHILADELPHIA EAGLES WON THE SUPER BOWL FOR THE first time in February 2018. Just seven months later, in September 2018, they played their first home game as Super Bowl Champions against the Atlanta Falcons. The first half was very sloppy and at halftime, the Eagles were trailing 6-3. The notoriously demanding Philadelphia fans serenaded their team with a chorus of boos on their way to the locker room. Did I mention that the Eagles were the defending Super Bowl Champions? What have you done for me lately?

When we think about God, we often ask the same question. Yes God, you are the Creator of all that is. Yes God, you sent your Son to die on a cross so that by believing I might have eternal life. But, really, "What have you done for me *lately?*" It should make us realize how much we take for granted the things that God *has* provided, while constantly complaining and griping about the things He hasn't. What has He provided for us that we take for granted? He gives us oxygen for our lungs, water for our bodies, rain for our crops, and food for our bellies. Most of us have clothes to wear, roofs over our heads, and have never missed a meal. In addition, He's given us a way out of our sin predicament. We can't get to heaven because of our sin, but God made a way. He sent His Son to die on a cross to pay the penalty for our sin. All we have to do is believe in Jesus for our salvation and our sins are forgiven. We spend eternity in heaven. Is that not enough?

Human nature being what it is, the answer is often, no. We always want more. We're always complaining. We forget to thank God for the prayer He did answer, and continue to worry about the prayer He hasn't yet answered. We want God to be a cosmic genie in a bottle who grants our every wish. Jesus said in John 6:25, "You seek me not because you saw signs, but because you ate of the loaves and were filled." What have you done for me lately? Life's difficulties draw us closer to Him and that's right where we need to be. Ultimately, we should want to be closer to Him not for what He can give to us, but because of who He is.

The Eagles came back and beat the Falcons and thousands of delirious Eagles fans cheered. What had the Eagles done for their fans lately? They won the game! But the players knew that the fans would turn on them the next time they played a bad first half. Let's not be like that toward God. I have been praying a very specific prayer for some time now and God has not yet said yes. I'm sure you have too. Let's love and worship God for who He is and not what He's done for us lately. John Piper has famously said, "God is most glorified in us when we are most satisfied in Him." Let's not ask, "What have you done for me lately?" Let's just be satisfied in Him.

REFLECTIONS:

- Think about whether you love God more for who He is or for what He provides.

- How can we be grateful rather than asking God, "What have You done for me lately?"

- Make a list of the ways God has provided for you throughout your life. Spend time each day this week thanking Him.

18

LIGHT OF THE WORLD

John 8:12: "I am the light of the world. Whoever follows me will not walk in darkness, but will have the Light of life."

MOST PEOPLE ARE ATTRACTED TO LIGHT. I KNOW I AM. I love a raging campfire, the full moon, and when planets shine their brightest. As I write, Venus has been putting on a show lately in the early morning hours. At Christmas, we love to tour the neighborhoods that have the best light displays. Light is a symbol of hope and goodness. After 9/11, New York City installed a huge light beam at the site of each building. Two parallel beams shone into the sky as far as you could see. The light was a symbol of hope. It showed that we will not be intimidated or defeated.

Our love affair with light shouldn't surprise us. God designed the human eye to work through the use of light. The pupil and cornea allow light to reach the retina. The retina receives images and transforms them into electric impulses that are carried by the optic nerve to the brain. The brain translates the impulses into images and so we see. God made us need to need light and He gave it to us to help us. For this reason, light is a familiar theme in the birth stories of Jesus and throughout the Bible. God used light to reveal, lead, and attract.

1. TO REVEAL: God used light to reveal good news to the shepherds keeping watch by night.

Luke 2:8-14: "In the same region there were *some* shepherds staying out in the fields and keeping watch over their flock by night. And an angel of the Lord suddenly stood before them, and the glory of the Lord shone around them; and they were terribly frightened. But the angel said to them, "Do not be afraid; for behold, I bring you good news of great joy which will be for all the people; for today in the city of David there has been born for you a Savior, who is Christ the Lord. This *will be* a sign for you: you will find a baby wrapped in cloths and lying in a manger." And suddenly there appeared with the angel a multitude of the heavenly host praising God and saying, "Glory to God in the highest, And on earth peace among men with whom He is pleased."

2. TO LEAD: God used light to lead the wise men to Jesus.

Matt 2:9: "After hearing the king, they went on their way, and the star, which they had seen in the east, went on before them until it came and stood over the place where the Child was."

3. TO ATTRACT: Jesus attracted the people to Himself using the metaphor of light in John 8:12: "I am

the light of the world. Whoever follows me will not walk in darkness, but will have the Light of life."

For those who have chosen light over darkness, at Christmas we celebrate that Jesus, the light of the world has come into the world. The Bible contrasts light with darkness repeatedly. It's a symbol of hope and goodness. Jesus represents both. How does Jesus represent HOPE? 1) Hope for today: We have a Savior who came into the world to help us in times of trouble. There is no trouble we experience that He did not experience, and no trouble that He won't be there to help us through. Ps. 46:1: "God is our refuge and strength, a very present help in trouble." 2) Hope in eternity: Because of His life and death, we know that we will spend eternity with Him.

How does Jesus represent goodness? Jesus has never done anything out of selfish motives. Never! Is that hard to believe? He was hungry, tired, and wanted to be alone at times, and yet at all times, everything He did was for the benefit of others. Who can live a life on earth and not have one selfish thought or action? Only Jesus. He wants us to spend eternity in heaven with Him. And not only us, but others too. He wants us to be focused on others as He was.

We can often be selfishly consumed with our own problems. The future is so uncertain. Who knows what's around the next bend? Because of Jesus' birth, we can look beyond ourselves and our problems. We are part of a larger story. Jesus is building His church. We are stones built on top of the foundation of the apostles as Paul said in Ephesians 2:20.

THERE ARE MORE STONES TO BE ADDED. OUR LARGER mission is not to worry about ourselves and our problems, but to be like Jesus, the Light of the world. Like light, we should be symbols of hope and goodness. We should reveal, lead, and attract people to Jesus so He may add them to the church. Jesus said John 5:14-16, "You are the light of the world. A city set on a hill cannot be hidden; nor does anyone light a lamp and put it under a basket, but on the lampstand, and it gives light to all who are in the house. Let your light shine before men in such a way that they may see your good works, and glorify your Father who is in heaven."

Jesus came into the world as light to give us peace, joy, and hope. Those who have chosen darkness look to the world for peace, hope, and joy. It won't be found there. The world is temporary and passing away, and so are our problems. Jesus offers us *eternal* peace, hope, and joy; not just in heaven but right now. We don't have to wait until heaven to experience peace, hope, and joy. Because of Christmas, we can have those things today, and we can share the light of Jesus with others. That's what the church does. We lead others to Christ. We show people the goodness of Jesus. We bring peace, hope, and joy to a world that greatly needs it, all because the light of Christ came into the world on Christmas day.

REFLECTIONS:

- What did Jesus mean when He said, "*You* are the light of the world?"

- List some ways you reveal, lead, and attract people in your sphere of influence to Christ?

19

A SPIRITUAL SONOGRAM

Psalm 139:1-2: "O LORD, You have searched me and known me. You know when I sit down and when I rise up; You understand my thought from afar."

WHEN DOCTORS WERE TREATING MOLLY'S CANCER, WE learned more than we ever wanted to know about the many ways that doctors can look inside the body. They can use MRI, sonogram, X-Ray, mammogram, needle biopsy, CT scan, and even surgery to reveal what is hidden. This is all for our benefit, even though it may be uncomfortable or painful. Doctors use all available technology, and like a game of hide-and-seek, they try to find what is hiding. As I thought about the technology that is needed to see our insides, I considered how God uses His omniscience to examine what's inside of us. He does it for our benefit, and it's often painful. Psalm 139:1-4: "O LORD, You have searched me and known me. You know when I sit down and when I rise up; You understand my thought from afar. You scrutinize my path and my lying down, and are intimately acquainted with all my ways. Even before there is a word on my tongue, Behold, O LORD, You know it all."

I find comfort in these words. God is omniscient. There is nothing outside of His knowledge. Down to every thought I think, God knows what no doctor on earth with the most advanced technology can ever know. Doctors can see our organs and tissues, but God can see our souls. If you don't know the goodness of God, these verses might seem terrifying. God knows our wicked thoughts. He knows if we are only doing good works so that others will praise us. He knows when we question His goodness or doubt His plans. He knows when we blatantly disobey Him. Rebellion against the king of the universe is high treason and deserves death.

Yet God still wants to help us. He knows our helplessness to stand before Him because of our sin. When we were unbelievers, God used His omniscience to expose our own sin to us, so that we would repent of it and trust in Jesus for our salvation. He also uses His omniscience to expose our sin so that we can fight it with the Holy Spirit's power. To believers, these verses are not scary at all because God is good.

We can't trust just *anyone* with our secrets. We fiercely protect our personal information so that identity thieves can't steal from us. We use our hands to shield the pin-pad when using our debit cards at the store. We guard our social security numbers. We know that there are bad guys on the internet who would rather empty our bank accounts than work. But our secrets are safe with

God. David trusted God so completely that at the end of Psalm 139:23-24, he asked God to do a multi-point inspection of his heart. Here's what he said: "Search me, O God, and know my heart; Try me and know my anxious thoughts; And see if there be any hurtful way in me, and lead me in the everlasting way." It's not a question of whether God knows the secrets and sinfulness of our hearts. He surely does. It's a question of whether we will hide from Him like Adam and Eve in the garden, or whether like David, we will turn to Him and allow Him to work in our lives to make us more like His Son.

It's not fun to go to the doctor and submit to various tests, but we do it because we know an ounce of prevention is worth a pound of cure. Avoiding the doctor may result in worse problems later. In the same way, God's spiritual inspection may not be pleasant, but if we avoid it, we may miss a diagnosis that could save us trouble later. Spiritual inspection, if we will submit to it, is done by our good God who is the Great Physician of our spiritual health too. So ask God to do a spiritual sonogram on your heart. He already knows what's there, but His examination is for your benefit. It's in submitting to Him and asking Him to fix what is found that healing takes place.

REFLECTIONS:

- What are your greatest fears when you have to submit to medical tests?

- What is the value of allowing God to examine your thoughts and motives?

- If God is all-knowing, why is it still important to ask Him to search your heart? What steps will you take to submit to God for spiritual examination and address the results?

20

TRUE SECURITY

**John 10:27-28: "My sheep listen to my voice; I know
them, and they follow me. I give them eternal life, and
they shall never perish; no one will snatch them out of
my hand."**

ONE OF THE COLLEGES THAT OUR SON APPLIED TO
personally interviewed applicants. I took him to the
admissions interview in downtown Dallas, on the 15th
floor of a beautiful building that covers a full city block.
The law firm whose name is etched in stone occupies the
entire building. The lobby floors are marble and its ceiling
is at least 50 feet high. There are two approximately 20 x
20-foot digital screens that display bright, colorful images
that transform from one into another like a kaleidoscope.
There is an abstract modern art sculpture that stretches
high into the air from the floor. I have no idea what it's
supposed to be. When I was practicing law, I had a few
occasions where I had to visit law firms like this one. To

their adversaries, they project a message that you are beneath them socially, financially, and in power and influence. Whatever sad little law firm you belong to, it's inferior to theirs. The hundreds of names on their letterhead are meant to intimidate you; to show that they can overwhelm you by their might, and to prove that they ooze money and dominance. To their clients, the message is that if you want to hire them, it's going to cost you plenty.

I remember being awed by the opulence of some of these big firms and wishing that I had bottomless resources to spend on marble floors, huge high-definition screens, and ridiculous sculptures. I didn't *need* any of those things. I earned a decent salary and my family was living comfortably. We had a nice house, reliable cars, took reasonable vacations, and had money in the bank. I knew that I would never have the obscene excess of those white-shoe law firms, but I still found pleasure and self-worth in our financial security. After we moved to Texas, I learned personally, through a series of unforeseen circumstances, that financial security is a very fragile thing. You can lose it in a hurry. The Great Depression, Enron, Bernie Madoff, and Covid-19 are just a few reminders that money can disappear. Binding your happiness and worth to wealth is like walking on thin ice and hoping that it won't give way.

If we can't have our security in wealth, what about our health? I'm in my 50's now, and in good health. I can still go out and run several miles. I don't get frustrated if I forget something upstairs and have to go back up to get it. I don't have any real physical limitations to be concerned about. I'm not 18 anymore, but I'm satisfied with my health. But good health is also fleeting. As many of us have experienced, it takes one call from our doctor to learn that scary diagnosis we feared is now a reality. We are all aging and are either dealing with a health problem or headed toward one. If we are grounding our peace and security in our health, it's only a matter of time before we will be robbed of it.

Relationships too may eventually disappoint us because the people we rely on are sinners. We may disappoint others too. The only One who is not tainted by sin is God, and that means that His promises are always true. God never guaranteed us financial security, or good health, or perfect relationships. But Jesus said in John 10:27-30: "My sheep listen to my voice; I know them, and they follow me. I give them eternal life, and they shall never perish; no one will snatch them out of my hand. My Father, who has given them to me, is greater than all; no one can snatch them out of my Father's hand. I and the Father are one."

Those are incredible, life-changing, eternity securing promises. When we believe the gospel, that Jesus Christ died for our sins and rose from the dead, and we trust in Him alone for our salvation, our eternal future is secure. Don't look for security in the things of this world. The longer we live, the more we learn that they are here today and gone tomorrow. Like the members of that prestigious law firm, we will all have our names etched in stone someday, on our gravestones. Whatever you are facing, true, lasting, eternal security is found only Jesus Christ.

Let your anchor sink deep into the bedrock of Jesus Christ and find your security there.

REFLECTIONS:

- Discuss a time when you lost something that made you feel secure.

- How has God taught you to place your trust in Him more than things?

- If you have trusted God with your eternity, why is it sometimes hard to trust Him with today?

HAVE YOU PEAKED?

1 Peter 2:2: "Like newborn babies, long for the pure milk of the word, so that by it you may grow up in respect to salvation."

AFTER WINNING THE MASTERS GOLF TOURNAMENT IN 2001, Tiger Woods held all four of golf's major titles, the U.S. Open, British Open, PGA, and the Masters at the same time. It was called the "Tiger Slam." In 1982, Michael Jackson released "Thriller," which became the best-selling album of all time. In 1741, Handel composed "Messiah" in just 24 days. Michelangelo completed the painting of the Sistine Chapel in 1512. What all of these people have in common is that their careers continued long after those signature moments. Probably none of them were thinking at the time that they had just achieved the peak of their athletic or creative genius.

When I was running marathons, I ran my fastest time when I was 32 years old. After that, my times were consistently (and drastically) slower. I didn't know that at 32 I had already peaked. It was only after subsequent marathons that I realized that I was on the backside of the hill. We all have a shelf-life for physical and creative ability. For physical ability, our prime may be in our twenties to thirties. Our shelf-life for creativity can be much longer, but still, it doesn't last forever.

Once we have passed our physical peak, we have to learn to readjust our goals. We can work out, eat well, and try to stay in our physical prime for as long as possible, but once it's gone, it's gone. That's why there is a Champions golf tour for professional golfers over fifty. In marathons, prizes are awarded according to age groups. Runners over the age of forty are called "Masters." For those of us well past our twenties and thirties, this may seem depressing. But I don't think it is. Your physical peak is not your life's peak. When I was 32, and in the best physical shape of my life, I wasn't even saved yet! So even though I had passed my physical prime, I thank God that the best days of my life were still ahead.

As we age and we begin to encounter physical limitations, we still possess the ability to grow spiritually. The issue is whether we still have the drive and desire. 1 Peter 2:2: "Like newborn babies, long for the pure milk of the word, so that by it you may grow up in respect to salvation." Notice the word "long." You must desire to grow spiritually to makes strides. We all have times when we feel spiritually stuck; as though it's one step forward and two steps back, or that we have hit a plateau that we can't seem to cross. A plateau is flat land at a higher elevation than the adjacent land. So by definition, even if we are stuck in a spiritual plateau, we are still on higher ground than the ground below. We had to climb to reach that plateau, and there is still higher ground, no matter how old we are.

While Paul was in prison waiting to be executed, he wrote to Timothy and asked him to bring his parchments. He wanted them because even though he lived as a prisoner in a dungeon, and he knew that his days were coming to an end, he still had the desire and ability to grow spiritually. Deut. 34:7 says, "Moses was one hundred and twenty years old when he died, his eye was not dim, nor his vigor abated." Moses and Paul did not allow age or physical limitations to impede their spiritual growth, and neither should we.

So here's the question: Have you peaked? Have you allowed yourself to stop growing spiritually? I hope you haven't. As long as God gives breath for our lungs, we have the opportunity to become more like Christ and to affect the world for God's kingdom. I'm past my physical prime, but I believe that my spiritual prime is yet to come. We have to make some concessions to our bodies as we age physically. But may we never surrender our minds and spirits to sloth and spiritual slackness while life remains in our bodies!

REFLECTIONS:

- Think about something you can't do as well as you did when you were younger. How does that make you feel?

- How can you know if you're growing spiritually?

- What habits can you start or develop to continue to grow spiritually? What benefits might you realize by developing those habits?

22

JUDGING BY GOD'S VALUE SYSTEM

Luke 15:6: "Rejoice with me, for I have found my sheep which was lost!"

WILL FULLER IS A WIDE RECEIVER FOR THE HOUSTON Texans. He played college football at the University of Notre Dame and by all accounts is a fine young man. Most importantly, during the 2018 season, he was the third wide receiver on my fantasy football team, usually scoring about 12 points a game for my team. In the middle of the season, Fuller landed awkwardly while catching a touchdown pass in a game against the Miami Dolphins. He had to be helped off the field. An MRI confirmed that he had torn his anterior cruciate ligament (ACL) and would miss the rest of the season. As a Christian pastor, of course, I immediately sent him a card and a fruit basket and wished him a speedy recovery. Actually, I did none of those things. I cut him from my team as quickly as possible and picked up the next best receiver I could find. With a healthy ACL, Will Fuller added value to my team. With a torn ACL, he did not.

Often our approach to people we meet is the same. We evaluate them to see how they could benefit us. Jesus didn't see people that way. In Luke Chapter 15, Jesus told three parables about how valuable each individual soul is to God. In the parable of the lost sheep, the shepherd left the 99 sheep in search of the one who was lost. When the shepherd found that lost sheep he rejoiced. Jesus said, "in the same way there will be more joy in heaven over one sinner who repents than over ninety-nine righteous people who need no repentance."

In the parable of the lost coin, a woman who had 10 coins swept her entire house because she had lost one. When she found it, she rejoiced. Jesus said, "in the same way, there is joy in the presence of the angels of God over one sinner who repents." In the parable of the prodigal son, a man's younger son asked his father for his share of the inheritance. Receiving it, he left for a foreign land where he squandered the inheritance by immoral living. When he repented and returned to his father, his father killed the fattened calf for him and threw a party. The father explained to his jealous and disgruntled older son that they had to rejoice and celebrate because the son that was lost had been found.

So who has the proper view of people, us or God? That's not a trick question. Let me suggest that God's view of people is proper. Where we make value judgments about how we can use people for our benefit, God sacrificed His Son for us to His great detriment. He loves and values each and every one of us, not because of what we can do for Him, but simply because He chooses to love us. In the same week that Will Fuller tore his ACL, a gunman shot and killed 11 Jews in a synagogue in Pittsburgh because of his hatred for them. Another man killed two elderly black people in a Kroger in Louisville because he hates black people. Their victims had no worth in the eyes and hearts of their assailants.

Until we see people the way God sees them, we will continue to marginalize them and evaluate them in terms of how they can benefit us. God valued each individual so much that He gave His Son for each one of us. God asks us to do so much less, and yet we fail daily. When Jesus was asked what is the greatest commandment, He said, "'You shall love the Lord your God with all your heart, and with all your soul, and with all your mind.' This is the great and foremost commandment. The second is like it, 'You shall love your neighbor as yourself'" (Matthew 22:37-39).

Can we love people as Jesus did? The first step is to be more concerned about *them* rather than what they can do for us. That's what Jesus did. Maybe I should have sent Will Fuller that fruit basket after all, but there are many people much closer to home who really need our help, love, or encouragement today. What will we do to love them as Jesus did?

REFLECTIONS:

- Compare and contrast how we assign value to people with how God does.

- Make a list of people who you value because of what they can do for you rather than who they are.

- How could you learn to value people as Jesus does?

23

THE PERFECT ADMISSIONS COMMITTEE

Romans 10:9: "If you confess with your mouth Jesus is Lord, and believe in your heart that God raised Him from the dead, you will be saved." (NIV)

FOR MANY HIGH SCHOOL STUDENTS, THE FIRST SEMESTER OF senior year means it's time to apply to college. We helped both of our kids apply, and the process is rigorous and monotonous. In addition to the application itself, a student must submit the application fee (of course), letters of recommendation from teachers, friends, and counselors, academic transcripts, SAT and ACT test scores, and a resume of additional achievements that would not appear on a transcript. Some schools even require students to submit a "mid-year" report and "final year" report from senior year to be sure that the student didn't tank senior year after the college application was submitted.

. . .

I READ A FEW ARTICLES ABOUT HOW SCHOOLS EVALUATE students for admission. Most schools have certain minimum GPA and test scores to be admitted, but once that hurdle is cleared, they have to slice the bologna pretty thin to make distinctions among very deserving applicants. There may be several kids with the same GPA and test scores, but one kid may be an Eagle Scout, another may have gone on mission trips, another may be captain of the band, another may be an entrepreneur, another may have invented something. In addition to all those criteria, schools are very sensitive about admitting the proper ratio of males and females, in-state and out-of-state students, and students of various ethnicities and religions.

If the admissions committee member who receives your application is impressed with you, he will fight for you at admissions committee meetings where final decisions are made. Meanwhile, other admissions counselors are fighting for their applicants, and there are only so many openings available. Schools are very secretive about their admissions process. You may have read about a lawsuit against Harvard University that alleged that its admissions process discriminates against Asian Americans. Harvard had to reveal some of its admissions process, which lawyers for the Asian American kids said clearly discriminated against them. The bottom line is that the college admissions process is not perfect. Those who judge are imperfect, fallible human beings with their own agendas, prejudices, and biases that affect their judgment. Mistakes happen. A more deserving kid may be rejected in favor of a less deserving kid. Life is not always fair and we need to get used to disappointment.

Not so with the Lord Jesus Christ. He is perfect, untainted by sin, prejudice, and bias. He judges with perfect righteousness. His judgments are incapable of being wrong. He does not hide behind nebulous admissions criteria when deciding who spends eternity in heaven and who does not. He asks one simple question. "Why should I let you into heaven?" When I was in high school and college, cheating on tests was rampant. (I doubt much has changed!) Our biology teacher used to give multiple-choice tests, and some wise guy in our class "found" the test before it was given, and passed it around. Some kids wrote the answers (a, b, c, d, or e), on their textbook covers as quarter notes on a musical staff. What looked like idle doodling to the unsuspecting teacher, was the answer key to the test! I'm not advocating, I'm just reporting. I personally would never be involved in such a scandal. ☺

We don't have to cheat on the test that Jesus gives us because the Bible gives us the answer to the question we will be asked. Romans 10:9 says "if you confess with your mouth Jesus is Lord, and believe in your heart that God raised Him from the dead, you will be saved." How gracious of God to give us the answer in advance! It's the easiest test you will ever take, aside from the fact that the proctor is the Creator of the whole universe! We often try to complicate the answer by injecting ourselves into it. We want to talk about the things *we* have done and why *we* deserve to get into heaven. That misses the whole point of the gospel. Let's not kid ourselves. We *don't* deserve to get into heaven. The gospel message is that God graciously allows us into heaven if we rely on the work of His Son, and not our own merit.

College applicants have to wait for schools to either admit or reject them based on their own achievements. I thank God that when it comes to salvation, we don't have to worry about beefing up our applications. There is nothing that we can do to make God love us any more or any less. When Jesus died on the cross, He said, "It is finished." Jesus finished the work that was required for any person to go to heaven. He died so we may live. Our salvation will not depend on the whims of some admissions committee, or some esoteric admissions criteria. When God asks us, "Why should I let you into heaven?" there is only one correct answer. "I have trusted in Christ alone for salvation." Knowing it means that we can live joyfully knowing that we will spend eternity with Him.

REFLECTIONS:

- Name a time when you felt unjustly judged by another. How did that make you feel?

- Do you still think the judgment was unfair? What could you have done to change the outcome?

- List your responses to knowing that God always judges perfectly.

24

YOU CALL THAT A BAGEL?

Exodus 16:2: "The whole congregation of the sons of Israel grumbled against Moses and Aaron in the wilderness."

MY FAMILY MOVED FROM NEW JERSEY TO THE DALLAS, Texas area in 2011. We love it here. It's in the Bible belt, the weather is great, no state income taxes, and real estate is affordable. As pastor of my church, I feel like I have the best job in the world! I have no regrets. But there are things I miss. I miss family and friends. I miss trips to the beach. The nearest beach to our house is five hours away. I miss good New York style pizza. I shudder at having to eat most pizza in Texas. Another thing I miss is a good bagel. I ate something one morning that the restaurant called a bagel, but was a pathetic imitation. It was like the two ends of a loaf of white bread with holes in the middle. No self-respecting north-easterner would have eaten it, but I was really hungry and there were no other options.

Sometimes it is easy to overlook all of our many blessings and complain about the things that we don't have. I would love to have a beach nearby, good pizza, and real bagels. But if that's all I have to complain about, then my life is pretty good. How about you? What do you complain about that draws your attention away from the many blessings in your life? I'm not talking about the real physical and emotional pain that life brings. I'm talking about minor daily complaints that sidetrack us from the joy of life.

In Exodus 14, God parted the Red Sea to allow the Israelites to escape from Pharaoh's army. Immediately after, in Exodus 15, the Israelites complained that there was no water in the desert, so God provided water. In Exodus 16:2-3, they complained again: "The whole congregation of the sons of Israel grumbled against Moses and Aaron in the wilderness. The sons of Israel said to them, 'Would that we had died by the Lord's hand in the land of Egypt, when we sat by the pots of meat, when we ate bread to the full; for you have brought us out into this wilderness to kill this whole assembly with hunger.'"

In less than two months from the parting of the Red Sea and their escape from Egypt, the Israelites had already become chronic complainers and revisionist historians. They had been slaves in Egypt. They were brutally and shamefully mistreated for 400 years! By the hand of God, they were led from their bondage in Egypt to freedom. The first thing they did was to grumble and complain about the things they didn't have. Their complaints would make you think that they were living in Egypt like kings in palaces, eating lobster and caviar, rather than as slaves making bricks without straw. We can imagine God shaking His head at their unfaithfulness, and yet, God provided meat for them to eat.

Complaining is the result of discontentment with what God has provided. It is the result of an unthankful heart, a lack of faith, and a focus on self rather than God and others. James 1:17, "every good thing and every perfect gift is from above." Everything we have is from God. We ought to give thanks for what we have rather than complaining about what we don't have. We ought to trust God to provide the things we need, and not complain that we don't have some of the things we want. We should be less focused on ourselves and more focused on God. Often, we complain because we are spending too much time thinking about ourselves and our own selfish preferences and desires, and not enough time thinking about the goodness of God, or the needs of others.

The best thing God has given us is His Son Jesus, who died on the cross for our sins so that we can have eternal life with Him. Let's not complain about what we don't have. If you believe in Jesus, you already have everything! Rejoice in that. Now, if anyone (not from the south) can recommend a place in Texas where I can find a decent bagel, I'm all ears!

REFLECTIONS:

- If you have ever moved, what are some of the things you miss from your old hometown?

- Would others say that you are the kind of person who sees the glass half-full or half-empty? Why?

- Start a gratitude journal by listing at least three things a day that you are thankful for.

25

SPIRITUAL ANEMIA

John 15:5. "I am the vine, you are the branches; he who abides in Me and I in him, he bears much fruit, for apart from Me you can do nothing."

IN THE FALL OF 2018, WE HAD A REAL SCARE WITH OUR DOG Bo. He had been laying around, not eating, and not moving when people came to the door. We knew that something was wrong. This dog would run through fire for a scrap of food. The veterinarian drew some blood, which revealed nothing worrisome. He gave him some steroids and an antibiotic. For a couple of days, he was his old self. Then he crashed again; no eating, no movement, just lying there. We took him back to the vet. That time the blood test revealed that Bo had anemia, which is a deficiency of red blood cells due to an auto-immune disease. His red blood cell count was significantly lower than just a few days before. The vet said that his chances of surviving were about 50/50. He prepared us for the worst. He said that Bo's body was producing red blood cells, but that his white blood cells were attacking them as though they were harmful invaders. The red blood cells carry oxygen to the rest of the body. Without them, Bo would die. The vet prescribed medication to help the red blood cells reach maturity. He asked us to come back in a week to see if the medication was working.

The problem of anemia, or the lack of red blood cells to carry oxygen to the body, reminds me of John 15:5. "I am the vine, you are the branches; he who abides in Me and I in him, he bears much fruit, for apart from Me you can do nothing." The branches draw life and power from the vine. When cut from the vine, the branches will surely die. Every time you buy your wife flowers, you hope they will appear to be alive for a week, even though apart from the life-giving vine, they are already dying. Jesus' disciples understood the metaphor. Jesus said that He is the vine. We are the branches. Our life and power are 100% derived from Jesus' life and power. Our ability to produce good fruit, that is, faith in God, making disciples, generosity toward others, and works that are pleasing to God is completely dependent on remaining in Jesus. That's why Jesus said so many times in John 15, "Abide in me." What does it mean to abide in Jesus and how do we do it?

The word abide means, "to remain." Remain in Him. We do it by reading the Bible daily, praying often, modeling our lives after Jesus' life, and communing with other Christians. These disciplines are the red blood cells that carry the oxygen of the life and power of Jesus to our desperate Spirits. I pray that as Christians, we have committed ourselves to more than just the elementary things of the faith. We know that Jesus died for our sins and rose from the dead. That's the gospel and it's the *entry point* into eternal life. But there is so much more! If we are going to have the abundant life that Jesus promised (John 10:10), we have to continue to grow in our faith. That happens as we nourish our bodies with the life-giving Word of God. Bo desperately needed those red blood cells to carry oxygen to the rest of his body. Without oxygen, his body could not live. Our spiritual lives are the same. If we neglect the Word, we too will die spiritually. Maybe not today, but over time, our spiritual lives will lose all vitality.

As for Bo, he recovered from his illness for a time. But we knew that it was a losing battle. He lived for a year and a half before we had to put him down in February 2020. Before he got sick, I had never spent a single second thinking about my red blood cells, even though I now understand how critical they are. I take them for granted because they have always done their job. We can't take our spiritual health for granted though. Our spiritual health depends on our cooperation with God, by remaining in Jesus as branches to the vine, so that we will develop into the men and women He wants us to be. We must be connected to the vine to have spiritual life. So don't neglect your spiritual health. Read your Bible daily, pray often, make it a habit to commune with other Christians, and watch those spiritual red blood cells grow!

REFLECTIONS:

- Think of a person who sets a good example for abiding in Christ. Explain why.

- How are you doing at abiding in Christ and what changes can you make?

- What are some practical steps you can take to remind you that growth is more about "being" in Him than "doing" for Him?

26

NEAR AND FAR

1 Corinthians 15:55: "O death, where is your victory? O death, where is your sting?"

DURING A RECENT RUN WITH A FRIEND, HE ASKED ME IF I look near, at the ground, or far, at the horizon, when I run. I said I tend to look near, at the next two or three sidewalk squares to be sure I don't trip and fall, although I do look up occasionally. He told me that he always looks far in the distance because he likes to reel in the horizon as he runs, but he looks down occasionally for safety's sake. For each of us, the answer was both, near and far. Good drivers should also always be looking near and far too. We need to be aware of immediate danger, and yet anticipate danger that could materialize ahead. We need to balance looking near and far.

In life, there is a balance between looking near and far as well. Time is a continuum of near and far events. Positively, we might have a vacation scheduled, tickets to a show, or an upcoming visit with family. There are also things in our near future that we can't wait to have behind us, like a dentist appointment, or jury duty, or a dentist appointment :). Life can be an endless series of wishing for the next unpleasantry to be behind us. As to things in the far future, I am really looking forward to becoming a grandparent, but not too soon! I'm very eager to see what God has planned for the church I pastor, but He will show us in His time. Of course, on the dread side of the coin, is that we will die someday. But believers don't have to dread death.

1 Corinthians 15:54-57: "But when this perishable will have put on the imperishable, and this mortal will have put on immortality, then will come about the saying that is written, 'Death is swallowed up in victory. O death, where is your victory? O death, where is your sting?' The sting of death is sin, and the power of sin is the law; but thanks be to God, who gives us the victory through our Lord Jesus Christ."

Our own deaths could happen before the sun sets today, or in the distant future. We are not promised one more day. But the good news is that whether near or far, our physical deaths are only the doorway to eternal life if we are believers in Jesus Christ as our savior. In that sense, Paul could write that death is swallowed up in the victory that Jesus Christ won for us on the cross. Jesus defeated sin. By dying on our behalf, Jesus took the penalty that we deserve for our sins. Anyone who has accepted Jesus Christ as Savior will not be condemned for his sin because Jesus has already paid for it. Jesus defeated death also. By rising from the grave, He proved that He has the power to raise us from the grave too.

Have you accepted Jesus Christ as your Savior? All you have to do is acknowledge that you are a sinner who has broken God's laws, but Jesus died for your sins and rose from the dead. Then turn from your sin and trust in Him for your salvation. Don't let another day pass without asking Jesus to forgive your sins. If you have already done so, you should be concerned for the salvation of your family and friends too. Death may be near or far, but with Jesus as our Savior, it really doesn't matter. We will be ushered into heaven where Jesus Himself will say, "Well done my good and faithful servant. Enter into the joy of your master."

REFLECTIONS:

- When is the last time you were excited about or dreaded an upcoming event? Why?

- Death is inevitable unless the Lord returns first. How does that make you feel?

- Read 1 Corinthians 2:9 and Rev. 21:3-4 and journal what heaven will be like. How does anticipating heaven affect how you will face present hardships and prepare for dying?

27

THE KING OF THE DUMP

Luke 12:25-26: "And which of you by worrying can add a single hour to his life's span? If then you cannot do even a very little thing, why do you worry about other matters?"

I RECENTLY SWITCHED FROM DIRECTV TO SPECTRUM. I HAD a very old TV that was not compatible with Spectrum's HDMI only cable boxes. So I bought a new TV and took the old one to the dump. You have to prove that you are a city resident with your driver's license and a copy of your most recent water bill to be allowed to dump. It was August, so technically, I should have brought July's water bill with me. I couldn't find the July bill, so I brought June's. Well, the King of the Dump raised Cain with me over it. "Did you look at the date on this water bill before you came? Do you know what, 'most recent' means?" I said, "Look, if it's that big of a deal, I'll go home and find the most current water bill." He then said, "I'll let you dump today, but be more careful in the future." I think he expected me to kiss his filthy boots at this display of grace.

This man was the king of the dump. It was his prerogative to enforce the rules strictly or to give grace. He clearly enjoyed his kingdom. I'm sure you all have had similar experiences. (Have you ever lived in a Homeowner's Association?)

Why is it that we want a kingdom so badly? I think it's because we have so little control in most areas of our lives that we desperately want to be in control of something. We try to control our health by exercising and eating right, but we could get a bad diagnosis any day. We try to manage our financial security by investing wisely, but the bottom could fall out of the stock market or real estate market without warning. We try to control what will happen to our assets after we die, but our kids might squander what we have worked hard to accumulate. We try to control our relationships by treating people well, but find that we have somehow unwittingly offended someone and we can't fix it. We realize that we are not in control of anything. We long for something that we can control with complete and unadulterated authority.

Jesus dismissed the idea that we are in control of anything. In Luke 12, in the great passage about controlling worry and anxiety said, "And which of you by worrying can add a single hour to his life's span? If then you cannot do even a very little thing, why do you worry about other matters?" We are not in control. God is sovereign and everything happens in accordance with His will and with His plans. I thank God for that. If we accept that God is good and omnipotent, then what do we have to fear? Usually, when I try to be king of my life, I get out ahead of God and I don't learn the lesson that He has planned for me in that moment. In doing things my way I miss the blessing He has for me and I make a dump out of my own life.

I tell myself that I don't want to be king of my life. I tell myself that I want to be a faithful subject of the only true King. But am I being honest? The only way to be a faithful subject is to surrender my life to the true King and let him rule it. That means allowing Him to use me and the circumstances around me however He wants. It means being thankful for suffering because of the lessons I learn from it. Most of us try so hard to maintain control, and then something happens that makes us realize that we never had control anyway.

God did not make me king of my life. The more I try to be king, the more I undermine His authority and get in the way of the work He wants to do through me. We have to surrender our lives to Him daily. People trying to lose weight start a new diet every morning. People who want to surrender their lives to God have to do it every morning too. Let's have the strength and wisdom through the power of the Holy Spirit to surrender to Him. He's a better King than we will ever be and He rules a greater Kingdom than we could ever build in our own power.

REFLECTIONS:

- Discuss a time when God showed you that you cannot control your circumstances.

- What does it mean to surrender your life to God?

- What are some things that you have not surrendered to God? Money, your children, health, physical appearance, or job security are some possible examples.

- What is your response to knowing that God is the King of the universe and is in control of everything that happens?

28

THE PROBLEM OF SCHADENFREUDE

Galatians 6:1: "Brothers *and sisters*, even if a person is caught in any wrongdoing, you who are spiritual are to restore such a person in a spirit of gentleness; *each one* looking to yourself, so that you are not tempted as well."

EVERY YEAR WHEN THE NFL SEASON BEGINS, LAS VEGAS posts the odds of which coach will be fired first. Can you believe that you can bet on such things? And that people do? As I thought about that, I thought about our apparent fascination in America with watching people fail and fall. I can't think of anything that receives more press coverage than the stories of failure, or stories of a fall from grace. Who can ever forget O.J. Simpson in the white Bronco, the Matt Lauer, Harvey Weinstein, Larry Nassar, and Jeffrey Epstein scandals, or Tonya Harding and Lance Armstrong? The very public moral failures of

Jim Baker, or Jimmy Swaggert are inscribed in our collective memory.

I don't know why these stories are so popular. Maybe it's what psychologists call "Schadenfreude," the emotion of taking pleasure in others' misfortune. Their explanation for schadenfreude is that these stories make us feel better about ourselves. We look for qualities in another that caused their failure, evaluate ourselves to be sure we don't have those same qualities. This makes us feel safe that the same things that happened to them can't happen to us. I think we have all probably experienced this emotion ourselves once or twice in our lives.

What this emotion ignores is that we are all sinners. James says whoever is guilty of breaking the law at any point is guilty of breaking the whole law. Jesus said if a man looks lustfully at another woman, he has already committed adultery. We all know that we fall short of God's standards, and we're thankful that we are not public figures whose failures will be exposed to the world on social media.

But God knows our failures even though the world may not. Paul warned us in Romans 12:3 "not to think more highly of himself than he ought to think; but to think so as to have sound judgment." If we do that, we will not rejoice in anyone else's failure. We will say, "There but for the grace of God go I." It could just as easily happen to us in the right (or wrong) circumstances. We should have compassion when someone falls into sin. Galatians 6 tells us to "restore such a one in a spirit of gentleness, each one looking to yourself so you will not be tempted." We must always be on guard or failure will come quickly.

As Christians, we don't bet on which coach will be fired first and then root against him. We don't rejoice when a celebrity who seemed to have it all crashed and burned. Schadenfreude is not Biblical. It's the opposite of the compassion that believers are to have for others, even if their own bad decisions led to their failures. After all, God is not done with them. Consider these examples: David committed reprehensible sins with Uriah and Bathsheba, yet God spared him. Paul was a murderer who became the greatest evangelist the world has ever known. John Mark deserted Paul and Barnabas on their second missionary journey in Pamphylia, but Paul later deemed him useful in ministry. Peter denied Christ three times but the Lord restored and commissioned him to go and make disciples.

God was not done with any of these men. Failure is one of the tools that God uses to draw people to Himself and to shape them for ministry. We don't know what the future holds for public figures who have fallen. We do know that as long as they live, God can still use them. If someone in our circle of influence fails, let's never be part of the problem by rejoicing in it. Let's be part of the solution by restoring one where we can Biblically, and helping him walk with Christ again.

And when we fail, even if no one knows it, realize that our story is not yet complete. God loves us, and the reason that we still have breath in our lungs is that God has a purpose for our lives. We repent and turn back to Him. There is grace at the cross for all who will come!

REFLECTIONS:

- Recall a time when you were pleased by the failure of another. Why?

- How would you feel if that person were your spouse, child, or best friend? What is the proper Biblical response to another's failure?

- What safeguards have you put in place to resist the temptation of sin?

29

BE RE-PURPOSED

John 5:24: "Truly, truly, I say to you, he who hears My word, and believes Him who sent Me, has eternal life, and does not come into judgment, but has passed out of death into life."

WHEN WE WERE SHOPPING FOR A HOUSE IN TEXAS, OUR realtor frequently used a term that we had never heard before. The term was "re-purpose." She would say things like, "If you don't like that light fixture in the foyer, you can "re-purpose" it in another room where it will be less conspicuous." Re-purposing simply means to use something in a different place or in a new way. I must confess that I am more of a "chucker" than a re-purposer. If I don't like the light fixture in the hallway, I'm not going to like it in a spare bedroom either, so I'll chuck it and get a new one.

I thank God that He's a re-purposer and not a chucker. Like many of you, I came to faith as an adult. I went to church as a kid, and I believed in God, but I didn't understand the gospel. As a teenager, I left the church and became an atheist. It was a full 20 years before God got my attention again, and gave me the grace to see that Jesus is God, and that He became a man to live a perfect life and to die for my sins. God raised Jesus from the dead to show that He has power over death. I understood by God's grace that to be raised to eternal life, all I needed to do was to trust in Jesus alone for my salvation.

Every Christian's story is basically the same. The details differ, but the theme is that God first draws us to Himself. He shows us our need for a Savior because of our sin, the beauty of Jesus and His sacrifice, and He causes us to believe. That's our salvation. Salvation means that we are spared from the wrath of God and eternity in hell, but it's so much more than that. John 5:24: "Truly, truly, I say to you, he who hears My word, and believes Him who sent Me, has eternal life, and does not come into judgment, but has passed out of death into life." Notice the use of the present tense. He who believes "has" eternal life now. Your eternity does not begin at your death. It began at your salvation and continues to eternity. Once you have been saved, God invites you to re-purpose your life for better, more productive use. 2 Corinthians 5:17: "Therefore if anyone is in Christ, he is a new creature; the old things passed away; behold, new things have come." We're the same and yet not the same. Somehow, we are made new, "re-purposed," and called to serve Him in a new way.

So the question is, how are you spending your eternity today? This life is not a waiting room for life in eternity.

God has prepared works for us to do (Eph. 2:10). This life is our daily opportunity to show our love and appreciation for the salvation that God has freely provided to us by serving Him. God wants you to re-purpose your life to further His kingdom. What skills do you have? What do you enjoy doing? Re-purpose yourself so that you use your gifts for the glory of God. All you have to do is to ask God to show you where He wants to use you. The Holy Spirit will encourage you to live for God. God has made you into something new, but it's up to you whether you will allow Him to use you.

It's so easy to let days, months, and years pass without ever attempting anything for God. But if you're not willing to risk anything for God, you won't accomplish anything for Him either. It's easy to settle for a comfortable life. It's in my nature and yours to seek comfort. But God didn't save us to make us comfortable. He saved us so that we would live re-purposed lives, showing the love of Jesus Christ to whoever we can, however we can. I need to remind myself of this every day because it is so easy to choose comfort and convenience over serving others. Let's choose to use the precious time and resources that God has given us to get busy living as redeemed and re-purposed instruments for His kingdom and His glory.

REFLECTIONS:

- Why do you think so many people choose personal comfort over serving others?

- Make a list of your passions, talents, and unique skills. How can God repurpose your skill set to serve or encourage people in the church?

- What benefits might result from serving others?

30

LOVE DOES

Luke 15:20: "But while he was still a long way off, his father saw him and felt compassion for him, and ran and embraced him and kissed him."

A COUPLE OF SUMMERS AGO, I READ A BOOK BY BOB GOFF called *Love Does*. The premise of the book is that God calls us to live with whimsical love. The word whimsy means extravagant, fanciful, or playful. To love whimsically means that sometimes you have to *do* things without worrying about the expense, or whether they make a whole lot of sense. Goff told story after story of how he has loved whimsically in his life, and I have to admit that I was jealous. He has lived a life of adventurous love. As we get older, we tend to become more cautious and conservative than we were in our youth. When I was younger, I didn't worry about anything, and that's not good either! But I never want to get to the point where I don't do *anything* for fear of whether I can afford it, or whether I have time, or who will feed my dog, or whether the house will be standing when I get home.

When the prodigal son returned home, Luke 15:20 says, "But while he was still a long way off, his father saw him and felt compassion for him, and ran and embraced him and kissed him." His father dressed his son in the finest clothes, put a ring on his finger, and killed the fattened calf to celebrate his return. That's whimsical love. It's extravagant, expensive, over the top love. It was so much more than the prodigal deserved, especially after the way he insulted his father by asking for his share of the inheritance while his father was still alive. I want to love like that father.

Right after I finished the book, I had an opportunity. My brother-in-law told me that Luke, his son, and our nephew, would be graduating from US Navy Boot Camp that Friday in Chicago. He had worked so hard to get there. About 5 weeks into the 8-week basic training program, they told him that he was not progressing well enough, and they added 3 more weeks to his basic training. He was devastated. The Navy rescheduled his graduation date to August 3, but the Navy always advises all the families to buy flight insurance if they plan to attend graduation because any trainee can be held back again at the last minute.

Molly and I had been talking about going up to Chicago for the graduation but as the days passed with no assurance that Luke would graduate, we gave up on the idea. But reading *Love Does* changed my thinking. There was no insurmountable reason why we couldn't go to Chicago on a moment's notice to be at his graduation. There were a bunch of practical reasons, but whimsical love doesn't list the reasons why we couldn't go. Instead, it figures out a way that we could go.

So we left that very afternoon. We drove 13 hours through the night to get to Chicago by the next morning. We went to the Chicago White Sox game at 1 pm. I've never been to the new stadium so I can check another stadium off my list. (I swear that's not the reason we went!) The Navy only allowed four tickets for admission per family, so Molly and I had to watch it on TV with some of the family. Later we all met for a nice celebration. It meant a lot to Luke that we made the effort. Then we drove back 13 hours the next day.

Does that seem crazy to you? When I was young, I would have done it without even thinking twice. Now that I am older and more cautious, I nearly talked myself out of it. But "love does." So we did it. We were so proud of Luke and we wanted to be there to share his moment with him. When Jesus died on the cross for our sins, that was not convenient. It was painful, humiliating, shameful, and worst of all, He was separated from His Father while He bore His Father's wrath for the sin of the world. If He had not done it, we could not be in heaven with Him someday. He had to pay the penalty for our sins. Love Does. That's how Jesus showed His expensive, extravagant, over-the-top love for us. Compared to that, what's a drive to Chicago and back to show our love for our nephew?

Reflections:

- Describe how God has shown His extravagant love to you.

- Relate a time when you showed extravagant love to another.

- How can you have more of a "love does" mindset in loving others? What might that look like for you?

31

MY NEW DINING ROOM

1 Kings 8:39: "For you, you only, know the hearts of all the sons of men."

MOST SUMMERS, MOLLY TRAVELS FOR A COUPLE OF WEEKS with the church where she works to help at a youth camp. Whenever she leaves me alone, I usually tackle a home improvement project to surprise her when she gets home. I'm sure she is afraid every time she leaves because I'm not the handiest guy in the world, and I could quickly get in over my head. This past summer I took on our hideous dining room. It started out innocently enough, just paint. But after I finished painting, I looked at the disgusting 18-year-old builder's grade carpet that my dog has used for things I don't even want to mention here and thought, "It's time for this to go." I peeled it back from the corner and thought hard about whether I could handle carpet removal and installation of a vinyl floor. I had recently helped install a new vinyl floor at our church, so I had some experience. I decided to go for it. I enlisted my son to help. It took us a couple of days, cost a little more than I had hoped, and came with a few challenges, but the finished product is really nice. I'm pleased with our work.

That got me thinking about the lengths that we will go to cover up things we don't like not only in our houses but in ourselves. We wear clothes that will best hide our flaws. Women (and some men!) wear makeup to cover blemishes. When dating, we try to hide the things about ourselves that might make our date run from the restaurant while we use the men's room. When we interview for jobs, we never admit the things about ourselves that we know will scare our employers off. We're careful about the things we post on social media. (Some of us should perhaps be more careful!) We go to great lengths to hide our real selves. We can get away with this to a certain extent because the people we are concealing our true selves from are not omniscient. They don't know what we are thinking. They don't know everything we've ever done. They don't know every wicked thought we've ever had.

Incredibly, our God knows all of these things and loves us anyway. 1 Kings 8:39: "For you, you only, know the hearts of all the sons of men." The context of that verse is Solomon's prayer of dedication of the temple. Solomon confessed Israel's sin and prayed that God would forgive. God knows every person's heart. God knows us better than we know ourselves and loves us anyway. How could He know our hearts and still love us?

Only because when God looks at those who have trusted Jesus for salvation, He chooses to see Jesus in all

His beauty, and not us in all of our sin. That's why the only way to receive the eternal love of God is to love His Son, Jesus. When I looked at my ugly dining room, I saw it exactly as it was. No flaw was hidden from my sight. When God looks at us, He sees us exactly as we are. No flaw is hidden from His sight. But how gracious is God that He would forgive our sin, as great as it is, when we choose to believe in His Son for the salvation of our souls. What a merciful and compassionate God we serve!

PS: Check out my new dining room!

REFLECTIONS:

- What is your gut reaction to understanding that God knows every thought you've ever had and everything you've ever done?

- How does it make you feel knowing that God loves you anyway?

- How can you cooperate with God to work together on your flaws?

32

WHAT A BUG BITE CAN TEACH US ABOUT SIN

Romans 8:13: "If you are living according to the flesh, you must die; but if by the Spirit you are putting to death the deeds of the body, you will live."

I WAS OUT FISHING WITH FRIENDS WHEN I FELT SOMETHING bite me on the wrist. I looked down and saw an ant there and flicked it off, but it immediately started itching, and I knew I was in trouble. I'm allergic to bees, but I learned on that day that I'm allergic to other bug bites too. I've been stung several times, so by now, I know the drill. Slowly the area around the bite started to swell. Then the swelling began to creep up my arm. Within a couple of hours, my hand looked like the Pillsbury dough boy's. With a bug bite, it's easy to diagnose the problem. I felt the bite and I saw the progress of the swelling as I reacted to the venom. (Check out the picture below). The antidote is a steroid shot, a relatively simple solution to the problem. After I got the shot, the swelling went down and my hand looked more like mine than an advertiser's cartoon. All of this got me to thinking about sin and salvation. Let me explain:

Sin gets into us like that ant's venom got into me. Sin is at the root of every problem we have in our lives. Unlike a bug bite, sin can be hard to diagnose, especially our own sin. It creeps into our lives like the swelling crept up my arm, slowly but surely, and if we don't get the antidote, our sin will do us harm. Satan entices us to sin, and he blinds our eyes so that we continue in it. If he's successful, we'll never make the connection that it's our sin that makes our lives so hard, and which also keeps us from heaven. Our problem is sin.

The antidote to sin is Jesus Christ. When Jesus died on the cross, He said, "It is finished" (John 19:30). That means that the payment for sin has been made. God will never punish us for our sin if we believe in Jesus for our salvation because the penalty is "paid in full." Jesus already paid it for us. That's wonderful news of course, but how does that help us *today* in our battle against sin? Romans 8:13 says, "If you are living according to the flesh, you must die; but if by the Spirit you are putting to death the deeds of the body, you will live."

Believers in Jesus Christ have the power to defeat sin because we have the Holy Spirit, the third person of the Trinity, living inside of us. If we want to stop sinning, we have to set our minds on what the Spirit desires. The will of God is not hard to discern. He wants us to live holy lives, lives of integrity, and high character. He wants us to stop worrying and to trust Him to provide for our needs. He wants us to share the love of Jesus with others. As we fill ourselves with the desires of the Spirit, the sin in our lives will decrease correspondingly.

If you have kids, you want them to be busy because you know that busyness keeps them out of trouble. God wants us to be busy doing His work in this world. We can't be sinning and doing His work at the same time. Sin is a choice. If I had been able to kill that bug before it had bitten me, I could have stopped that venom from getting into me. If we choose to kill sin before it gets into us, we will be spared so much suffering and hardship.

Let's be filled with the Holy Spirit; let's get about doing God's work. We will never be completely free of sin, but that should still be our goal. We must be on the alert for sin trying to creep into our lives.

REFLECTIONS:

- Describe a time when sin crept into your life like venom into your bloodstream.

- What effects did you suffer as a result?

- List some defenses you can put in place to stop sin from poisoning your life.

33

THE ARMADILLO'S WORLD,
AND MINE

1 Peter 2:11: "Beloved, I urge you as aliens and strangers to abstain from fleshly lusts which wage war against the soul."

THE OTHER MORNING I WAS WALKING ON THE GOLF COURSE as I do most mornings. As I turned around a little bend, there was an armadillo about 20 yards ahead of me, munching on bugs, and not noticing me at all. As I came closer, he heard me. He turned and looked at me, trying to judge if I was friend or foe. He must have decided not to take any chances. He slinked closer to the woods and then darted into them. I wanted to follow him, but they were dense. With my history of bug bites followed by emergency room visits, I decided to leave him alone.

My world is out in the open, on a concrete path around a man-made golf course where people walk, ride bikes and play golf. His world is in the forest, away from people and other creatures that mean him harm. While out in the open, he was in my world and uncomfortable there. His sanctuary is the protection of the trees. Had I crossed followed him, I would have left my world and entered his, where bugs and snakes bite, and unseen danger lurks all around. Which got me thinking…

Why is it so hard for us as Christians to feel at home in the world? It's because we see sin all around us. It constantly tempts us to do what we know is wrong. Like the armadillo out in the open, or me in the forest, it's uncomfortable and unnatural for Christians to live in a world that does not fit Christ's desire for our holiness. That's why 1 Peter 2 says that we are "strangers and aliens in this world," and encourages us to "abstain from fleshly lusts that wage war against our souls." Is it hard to abstain from fleshly lusts? Of course it is. Sin is fun for a time. Fleshly lusts are enticing. Satan tempts us to surrender to them. It's hard to live in this world as Christians because the opportunity to gratify our fleshly lusts constantly bombards us.

Why is it that though we live here, we feel like aliens and strangers? It's because somewhere in the depths of our souls, we Christians know that this world is not our ultimate home. Hebrews 13:14 says, "For here we do not have a lasting city, but we are seeking the city which is to come." We know that Jesus is preparing a place for us so that where He is, we will be also (John 14:2-3). One day, we will inhabit that dwelling place that the Lord has prepared for us. As Paul said in Phil 3:20, "For our citizenship is in heaven, from which also we eagerly wait for a Savior, the Lord Jesus Christ."

. . .

AS WE LIVE IN THIS WORLD, WE WILL BE TEMPTED EVERY DAY to accept what it offers. Not a day will pass that we will not have the opportunity to indulge in every manner of sin. As this world falls further into moral decay, we must "walk in a manner worthy of the calling with which you have been called." (Eph. 4:1), and to "not let sin reign in your mortal body so that you obey its lusts, and do not go on presenting the members of your body to sin as instruments of unrighteousness; but present yourselves to God as those alive from the dead, and your members as instruments of righteousness to God." (Rom. 6:12-13). We *can* do this with the Lord's help by the power of the Holy Spirit (Rom. 8:9-12). We *can* resist the temptation to sin (1 Cor. 10:13). We *can* live in this world and not become part of it (1 John 2:15-16).

That armadillo could come out of the forest for a brief time. And I may have been able to walk in the trees for a little while. But we are not suited to live in each other's world. The same is true of disciples of Christ trying to live where sin is all around us. True disciples of Christ have to avoid the sin that tempts us and means to do us harm. For now, God has allowed Satan some dominion over the earth, and Satan means to destroy us with the temptations of it. Be careful to avoid his snares. There's nothing but trouble ahead when you allow yourself to enter his world.

REFLECTIONS:

- Describe a time when you felt out of place.

- Why is it that Christians feel discomfort in the world?

- What are some ways that you can influence the world for good, rather than allowing the world to influence you?

LIFE WITHOUT MY MAC

Psalm 42:1: "As the deer pants for the water brooks, so my soul pants for you O God."

LAST YEAR THE KEYS ON THE RIGHT SIDE OF THE KEYBOARD on my Mac stopped working. I had to take it to the Apple Store for service. They said that the problem was that the battery located under the keys had swollen and needed to be replaced. I was without the computer for a week while they worked on it. When I got it back, they had replaced the battery and the keyboard, but the keys still did not work. I brought it back again. After another ten days, they had replaced the battery and the keyboard a second time, but the keys still didn't work. I was beyond frustrated. I *need* my computer! I called Apple support to complain and let them know that maybe the problem wasn't the battery and keyboard. They figured out that it must be a software problem. After a combined five hours on the phone with them, they finally diagnosed the problem and fixed it.

After three weeks without my computer, I was back in business.

Here are some things that I learned:

1. I need to learn to be more dependent on the Lord than I am on my computer. Jesus is everything I need. Psalm 42 says, "As the deer pants for the water brooks, so my soul pants for you O God." While without my computer, my soul was thirsting for it more than it was thirsting for God. I rely on my computer every hour, every day. It's physical, tangible, and helps me get my work done. I almost can't function without it. How I need to learn that the same is true of Jesus! I need Him every day, every hour. He is my life, my breath, and I can't function without Him.

2. My problems are relatively minor. There are millions of people in the world who don't have clean water to drink or food to eat, and I was whining like a petulant child because my Mac was in the shop and I had to borrow a PC. The horror!! We are so materially wealthy that sometimes we invent things to complain about. I'm not saying that some of us don't have real problems, but most of the things we complain about would be laughable to much of the rest of the world. Griping about invented problems is nothing new. In Numbers 11, after God rescued the Israelites from 400 years of bondage in Egypt, they complained about having to eat manna day after day. I took time today to ask forgiveness for my selfishness and ignorance of the real problems in the world, and I thanked God that He has provided for my every need.

3. I NEED TO WORK ON MY PATIENCE. THIS IS NOT A NEW revelation to me. God keeps giving me opportunities. I can imagine Him smiling and shaking His head at me when I fail yet again. I am not so eagerly awaiting my next test! All things are under His control and happen according to His perfect timing. Psalm 33:20 says, "Our soul waits for the Lord; He is our help and our shield." I know it and still am poor at waiting on the Lord. I'm not just talking about computers, but every prayer I am waiting for the Lord to answer. Can you relate?

I hope that you had a little chuckle at my trivial problem, but I also hope you can see a bit of yourself in it. Jesus is our Lord and Savior. By His wounds we have been saved. When we value anything more than Him, or complain that He has not provided, or are not willing to trust His timing, we do Him a disservice. May we let God be God and be content with His provision!

REFLECTIONS:

- Imagine that Starbucks, Amazon, or your favorite company instantly disappeared? How would you handle that?

- Would other people say you are a patient person? Why or why not? How can you learn to develop more patience?

- What habits can you develop to help you yearn for God as much as you depend on material things?

35

LESSONS FROM THE DMV

Colossians 3:23: "Whatever you do, do your work heartily, as for the Lord rather than men, knowing that from the Lord you will receive the inheritance."

IF THERE IS ANYTHING THAT APPROACHES MY DREAD OF going to the dentist, a trip to the Division of Motor Vehicles would have to be right up there. But my daughter needed to renew her driver's license, so off we went. While we waited, I noticed that one of the clerks was especially friendly, funny, and engaging to his patrons. When my daughter's turn came, he was the one who called her. He asked her questions to get to know her and showed genuine interest in her. It reminded me of Colossians 3:23: "Whatever you do, do your work heartily, as for the Lord rather than men, knowing that from the Lord you will receive the inheritance." Whether we are CEO of a Fortune 500 company or an employee at

DMV, we can work heartily for the Lord. This man exemplified that principle.

He took time to get to know people that he'll probably never see again. After he renewed my daughter's license, he said, "I'll see you in 6 years." That was a sweet way to end their business and it made us smile. It's not often that you leave DMV smiling! If taking time to build a relationship in a five-minute business transaction can have that kind of effect, how much greater a mark can we make if we take time to build relationships with people we see every day? How could we influence our neighbors, co-workers, friends, and family if we were willing to invest in our relationships with them?

I saw a man that was content in his work. Ecclesiastes 5:18-19 says: "Here is what I have seen to be good and fitting: to eat, to drink and enjoy oneself in all one's labor in which he toils under the sun during the few years of his life which God has given him; for this is his reward." No matter what God has given us to do, it is a gift from Him that we ought to do with joy and enthusiasm.

God never said, "do your work heartily *if you like your work*," or "enjoy oneself in your labor *if you like your work*." He wants us to do what we do as unto Him and to serve others as we would serve Him. You may not love your job, and even most people who like their jobs have bad days. God calls us to serve Him and serve others, and shine the light that He has given us to the world, and that includes in our work.

Let's try to view all our interactions as opportunities to be salt and light in a dark world. You never know who you may influence.

REFLECTIONS:

- Remember a time when you received excellent customer service. What made the experience so good?

- List the things you like about your work. How can you make your work more than just a paycheck?

- If you don't work outside of the home, how can you make your daily interactions more meaningful?

36

THE FATE OF A BUNNY

Romans 8:31: "If God is for us, who can be against us?"

I WENT OUT FOR MY MORNING WALK TODAY WHILE IT WAS still dark. I could see headlights coming up from behind me, and then right in front of me a little bunny darted past and ran into the street. My first thought was "Oh no! Run bunny, run!" I was rooting for the bunny. I didn't want him to get smeared by the oncoming car. Then I thought, "why should I care what happens to that bunny?" I didn't create that bunny. I don't love that bunny, and yet I still felt compassion for him. I might have felt different if it was a rat or a snake!

An evolutionist would have no answer to the question of why should we care about the bunny. To an evolutionist, there is no God, life evolved from the slime by chance, life on earth is ultimately meaningless, and only the fittest will survive to pass on their genes. An evolutionist would say that if the bunny dies, it's because it's too stupid to wait for the car to pass. His death means that he will not pass his stupid gene onto other bunnies, which helps the bunny gene pool. That's a very clinical way to look at the bunny's fate. Only the most hardened evolutionist would root against, or be indifferent to the bunny. Why? Because we are *all* made in the image of God and God has given us hearts like His, hearts of compassion.

Now if we can be compassionate to a bunny that we didn't create, and whose survival doesn't benefit us, a creature in whom we have no investment, imagine how God feels about us. God created us. He loves us. He sent His Son to die for us to pay the penalty that we deserved for our sins so that we can be with him in heaven. Of course, God is rooting for us a million times more than I was rooting for that bunny. Romans 8:31-32: "What, then, shall we say in response to these things? If God is for us, who can be against us? He who did not spare his own Son, but gave him up for us all—how will he not also, along with him, graciously give us all things?"

Isn't it a glorious thing to know that God is for you? God is rooting for you! He is not indifferent to you. He wants intimacy with the world and the people He created. He loves you and cares for you more than you could ever understand. He wants you to be encouraged. A friend of mine gave me a great quote. He said, "discouragement never comes from God." And that's true.

Discouragement is a weapon that Satan uses to hold us down, to keep our eyes and thoughts on ourselves so that we will not worship God. If God is for us, who can be against us? We should be encouraged, and take time to lift the spirits of others who may not share our joy!

P.S. Happy ending: the bunny made it across the road!

REFLECTIONS:

- In what ways has God shown you that He is "for you?"

- Give an example of how God showed that He wants the best for you even after something bad happened?

- What is your response to the truth that God is "for you?" How can you encourage others with that truth?

37

LEARNING FROM A LABRADOR

Romans 8:32: "He who did not spare His own Son, but delivered Him over for us all, how will He not also with Him freely give us all things?"

I'VE ALREADY MENTIONED OUR CHOCOLATE LABRADOR WHO was named Boaz. The name "Boaz" means, "There is strength in him." He was an aptly named dog. He was a 100-pound, indestructible, food-seeking, eating machine. We called him "Bo." We bought 40-pound bags of dog food and I was often tempted to dump the whole bag on the floor to see if he could take it down. I'd like his chances.

One night, I was in the kitchen cutting up the last of a rotisserie chicken, and there was Bo, right by my side, hoping for any morsel to fall to the floor so he could pounce on it. We eat rotisserie chicken about once a week, and he learned to recognize the container. He would stand at attention knowing that some chicken skin was probably coming his way. There's always some good gristle near the skeleton too, but I have to be careful that no small bones get mixed up with the meat or he could choke. Bo wanted me to throw the whole chicken on the floor and let him have at it. I couldn't do that because I know what's best for him. (You may say that chicken skin is not the best for him either, but don't be a party pooper!)

As I was thinking about that, I thought about how we pray. Our prayers are usually asking God to relieve some form of pain or suffering, or asking Him to provide us with something we do not have. We want God to give us everything we ask for immediately. But God knows better. He knows that when we are living in unbridled prosperity, we tend to forget Him and drift away in self-contentment. Being disconnected from God is unhealthy for us. It's often our need that keeps us close to Him. Not only that, but there are lessons to be learned while we wait on God that we would miss if He granted our every wish like a genie in a bottle.

I've heard it said that God answers our prayers based on what we would have asked for if we knew everything that He knows. I like that. Since I'm not omniscient, I can't know everything God knows, so I don't know what's best for me. But since I know that God is good and that He loves me, I know that He will give me what is best for me in His timing. If Bo knew what was best for him, he wouldn't be begging for me to toss him the whole chicken carcass. If I knew what was best for me, I wouldn't be asking for God to fix all my problems at once. The blessing is often in the waiting.

HERE'S ANOTHER THING I NOTICED AS I GAVE BO THE scraps. After he devoured the chicken skin, he did not lick my leg appreciatively or otherwise rub up on me to show his eternal gratitude at this bounty of blessing. No, he continued to look at me like, "That's it? Come on, what else is there?!" We do the same with God. Many times, when God has answered my prayer and fixed a problem that I could not solve, five minutes doesn't pass before I complain about the next problem. I would forget to thank God, and immediately allow the next thing to consume me. I'm sure that I disappoint God when I have that attitude. I need to remember to thank Him for His daily and abundant blessings. Every one of them is a gift of pure grace. He owes me nothing but gives me so much. Yet I act like I am entitled to more, as though He owes me something.

Remember that God gave His Son to die a shameful and agonizing death on a cross to pay for our sins so we could have eternal life if we will believe in Him for our salvation. As if that wasn't enough, Romans 8:32 says, "He who did not spare His own Son, but delivered Him over for us all, how will He not also with Him freely give us all things?" He will not withhold any good thing from us, but let's allow Him to decide when we should have it. He knows what's best for us. In the meantime, let's remember to thank Him for the blessings He has already given, and don't miss the lessons that He has for us while we wait.

REFLECTIONS:

- What have you been asking God for that He has not yet given to you? Have you considered that it may be for your benefit that He withholds it or delays it?

- Describe a time when you experienced God's blessing while you waited on His timing.

- Consider that God did not spare His own Son but gave Him up for us. How can keeping that in mind give you peace while you wait for God to answer prayer?

38

SCRAMBLED EGGS AND CHRISTIAN MATURITY

2 Corinthians 1:8-9: "We do not want you to be uninformed, brothers and sisters, about the troubles we experienced in the province of Asia. We were under great pressure, far beyond our ability to endure, so that we despaired of life itself." (NIV)

I LOVE EGGS. I EAT LOTS OF THEM. I LIKE THEM OVER EASY, but scrambled is my favorite. I prefer them loose, moist, and fluffy, with salt and pepper. If I feel like throwing my health to the wind, I add cheddar cheese and ham. As I was making my scrambled eggs one morning, I realized that my simple breakfast is a metaphor for life as a Christian. To cook scrambled eggs, you have to break the shell, exposing the egg inside. Then beat those eggs with a fork so that the yolk breaks and mixes with the white. Next, you pour the liquid eggs into a pan, exposing them to extreme pressure, the external source of intense heat. You push them around the pan with a spatula until they become solid and firm. Then you take them off the fire.

The Christian walk is like scrambled eggs. Like the egg, so often we are broken, beaten, and exposed to the extreme pressure from the world that comes in various forms. It can be work expectations, time crunch, financial struggles, health concerns, relational conflict. How can we manage all of this pressure?

2 Corinthians 1:8-9 says, "We do not want you to be uninformed, brothers and sisters, about the troubles we experienced in the province of Asia. We were under great pressure, far beyond our ability to endure, so that we despaired of life itself. Indeed, we felt we had received the sentence of death. But this happened that we might not rely on ourselves but on God, who raises the dead."

Paul sounds like he was on the verge of a nervous breakdown when he wrote this. The stress was beyond what he could handle. He thought that he was about to die. God allowed Paul to be broken and beaten, and to face extreme heat. When God rescued him, Paul's faith became solid and firm like my scrambled eggs. Paul learned to trust God and then God took him off of the fire.

When we face the pressures of life, we must know and embrace the truth that God has a reason for them. Nothing can happen to us without God allowing it, and God doesn't waste anything that He permits. As we face the hardships of life, whatever their source, we should be encouraged, not discouraged. If we can look at life from God's perspective, we will see as Paul did, that our afflictions are momentary compared to the eternal weight of glory that awaits us in heaven (2 Cor. 4:17). Pressure and stress last for a time, but God uses them to solidify our faith. Let's trust God more in our circumstances as we read His Word, pray, and develop our relationship with Him. Even when we are broken, beaten, and exposed to tremendous pressure, we have a God in heaven who loves us, who sent Jesus to die for us, and whose plans for us are good. May the hardship that God allows strengthen your faith as you trust in Him today.

REFLECTIONS:

- Describe a time when you felt intense pressure or stress.

- What are some of the things God has taught you in times of hardship?

- When you go through a crisis, how can you learn to focus on what God wants to accomplish through it?

39

YOU'VE GOT TO BE "SWOONING" ME!

Acts 22:8: "'Who are you, Lord?' I asked. "'I am Jesus of Nazareth, whom you are persecuting,' he replied." (NIV)

I HEARD A BUZZING SOUND NEAR THE WINDOW IN MY OFFICE this morning and saw that it was a bee. As I've mentioned, I am quite allergic to bees. If I get stung, I have to go right to the ER for a steroid injection. Since I don't like to go to the ER for steroid injections, I closed the blinds, trapping the bee between them and the window. I listened for the buzz and then crushed the bee between my blinds and the window with a very heavy book. The bee fell to the windowsill, still moving and buzzing a bit. So I swept him to the floor and smashed him with the book again. The bee was stone dead. Then I picked him up with a wad of toilet paper and flushed him down the toilet. Then I flushed again, and watched for a minute, just in case.

Easter is Christianity's most sacred holiday and the basis of our faith. Jesus died for our sins and was raised from the dead, and if we believe in Him for our salvation, we too will be raised to eternal life with Him in heaven. That's the significance of Easter. But before there could be an Easter resurrection, Jesus had to die and be buried.

Amazingly, despite all that the Roman soldiers did to Jesus, some argue that Jesus wasn't raised from the dead because He didn't actually die on the cross. Is that possible? Here's what Jesus endured. They beat Him beyond recognition, scourged Him with whips embedded with pieces of stone and bone that would tear His flesh from His body. They forced Him to wear a crown of thorns, and carry His cross to the place of crucifixion. They nailed Him to that cross and allowed Him to hang there for 6 hours until he stopped breathing. The centurion stabbed him in the side with a spear so that blood and water flowed from the wound, just to be sure He was dead. Then Pilate gave the body to Joseph of Arimathea, who wrapped Him in linens and placed Him in a cold dark tomb. And yet, some argue, Jesus survived.

Between Friday night when He was buried and Sunday morning, so the argument goes, the cool air in the tomb combined with a day of rest revived Him. He recovered, wiggled out of His grave clothes, rolled the massive stone away, and left the tomb. He accomplished all of this without functioning hands and feet because the crucifixion spikes severed his nerves and tendons. He left the tomb undetected by the Roman guards who were stationed outside for the very purpose of guarding the body under the penalty of death if they failed.

THIS FAR-FETCHED FANTASY IS KNOWN AS THE SWOON theory. Its proponents say that medical knowledge at the time was not what it is today, so the executioners and witnesses all mistakenly believed that Jesus was dead. He didn't die, he only "swooned," meaning that He merely fell unconscious. I don't know about you, but I find this explanation a whole lot harder to believe than the resurrection. Some critics will go to great lengths to deny a historical fact. When I was investigating the Christian faith, the fact that Jesus' tomb was empty was the tipping point. I looked for any other plausible explanation. If the Swoon theory is the best argument that critics could make, then arguments against the resurrection are extremely weak. When Jesus was laid in the tomb, He was dead. There is no way Jesus could have survived what He endured.

Christianity is a religion based on faith, but it's also a religion based on facts. You need some facts to have faith. The Apostle Paul should know. While looking for Christians to arrest, Paul saw the risen Jesus. Paul testified in Acts 22:7-8: "Suddenly a bright light from heaven flashed around me. I fell to the ground and heard a voice say to me, 'Saul! Saul! Why do you persecute me?' 'Who are you, Lord?' I asked.' 'I am Jesus of Nazareth, whom you are persecuting,' he replied."

Then Paul traveled for the next 30 years preaching the gospel, and enduring beatings, whippings, torture, stoning, shipwreck, and finally martyrdom for his trouble. The only explanation for Paul's changed life is that he saw the risen Lord alive. That bee I killed did not come back to life. Jesus did. The evidence is too compelling to deny. If you struggle with belief, investigate the resurrection for yourself, and see if the evidence leads you to faith.

REFLECTIONS:

- What proof would you give to someone who doubts that the resurrection ever happened?

- How does the proof of Jesus' resurrection strengthen your faith?

- What does Jesus' resurrection mean for you personally?

40

A DIFFERENT KIND OF SELECTION SHOW

John 3:16: "For God so loved the world, that He gave His only begotten Son, that whoever believes in Him shall not perish, but have eternal life."

As you know by now, I am a big sports fan. College basketball is my favorite. I am especially passionate about my North Carolina Tar Heels. They won the NCAA Tournament in 2017, but in 2018, I watched in disbelief as underdog Texas A&M thumped them in the second round.

The regular season of college basketball is about four months long. Each game is important because teams need to build a resume that's impressive enough that the NCAA Tournament selection committee will invite them to participate in the tournament. Every year several teams are "on the bubble." That means that the team's resume is not too impressive, either because it has an average record, or it hasn't beaten many quality opponents. Bubble teams are in danger of not being selected by the committee. A school does not want to be "on the bubble" and leave its fate to the judgment of a fickle and fallible committee. It wants to be sure to win its way into the tournament.

The teams that the committee invites into the tournament are placed in four regions, and "seeded" according to the strength of the season they had. The best team in each region receives the number 1 seed. The weakest team in each region is seeded 16th. It's a single-elimination format, lose and go home. A team has to win six games in a row to win the tournament and only one team can do it. One by one, teams are eliminated until the 63rd and final game of the tournament, when only one team is left standing. The team that wins six games in a row against the toughest competition possible takes home the trophy.

Here's where I am going with all of this. Unlike how we get to heaven, a team has to work to get into the tournament and work to stay in, and in the end, only one team has done enough work to claim the trophy.

By comparison, Christianity has no "selection show." We don't "earn" our way into Christianity by our work (Eph. 2:8-9). We don't have to beat anyone or have a better resume than anyone to get in. In fact, we don't worry about *our* resume at all. We rely on Jesus' resume. Jesus Christ died for our sins and rose from the dead. All we need to do is to trust in Him for our salvation, and we are in. There are no people who are "on the bubble." We either believe, and are in, or we don't believe and we are out. There is no limit on the number of people who can get in. All are invited (John 3:16), so we don't have to worry about a fickle and fallible committee. We have a perfect, holy, and just judge who knows our hearts and gladly allows us into heaven on the strength of Jesus' resume, not ours.

Once we are in, we don't have to beat anyone to stay in. Christ died once to secure our salvation for all eternity (John 10:30). We cannot lose our salvation, so we don't have to worry about getting knocked out by some better team like the "North Carolina Billy Grahams." Once in, we don't chase a gleaming gold trophy that says we are worthy champions. We are all winners in God's eyes when we believe. We receive a gleaming gold crown when we enter heaven (Rev. 2:10; James 1:12). But we don't seek the crown. We don't even keep our crown. We will cast our crown back to our Savior who earned it for us in the first place (Rev. 4:10).

Christianity is a grace-based religion that seeks a relationship with Christ as its goal. I will always love the NCAA tournament, but I am less interested once my Heels are eliminated. I thank God for a salvation so great that it cannot be earned and cannot be lost, even if I have a dreadful day, as my Heels had against Texas A&M.

REFLECTIONS:

- How does it make you feel to know that you don't have to compete with others to gain salvation?

- Describe your response to knowing that once you have trusted in Jesus, you can never lose your salvation?

- How can you show your gratitude to Jesus for selecting you to go to heaven?

41

FENCE POSTS

Acts 9:27: "But Barnabas took hold of him and brought him to the apostles and described to them how he had seen the Lord on the road, and that He had talked to him, and how at Damascus he had spoken out boldly in the name of Jesus."

THERE'S A CHAIN-LINK FENCE AROUND A BASEBALL diamond that I pass on my morning walks. A chain-link fence has steel posts to support it every 6-8 feet. The fence is strongest at the fence post. One foot away from the post, the fence is a little weaker. Another foot away from the post and the fence is weaker still. It's weakest in the middle. A fence must be supported by posts or it will collapse.

If you have ever pushed a chain-link fence at the fence post, you know that you can't move it. But between the posts, there is a lot more "give" in the fence. I used to climb chain link fences all the time as a kid. It took a lot more than a fence to keep me out of the baseball field! If you remember climbing chain link fences as a kid, you always climbed the fence at the post because that's where the fence was the strongest and provided the most support.

Looking at that fence got me thinking about our walk with Christ. When we are regularly reading our Bibles and spending time with God, we are like the fence near the post. We are strong, supported, and even immovable. The same happens when we spend time with other Christians who encourage us and build us up. When we fall out of the habit of reading our Bibles and regular prayer or become isolated from other believers who encourage us and build us up, we drift from the fence post. We become weak and unsupported. There is "give" in our spiritual lives.

Barnabas was known as an encourager. In fact, his name means, "Son of Encouragement." In Acts 4, he was the first one mentioned who sold his property and donated the money to the poor. In Acts 9, when all of the apostles were afraid to meet Paul, Barnabas vouched for him that his conversion was genuine. In Acts 11, Barnabas helped collect money for the poor in Jerusalem and deliver it from Antioch. After John Mark abandoned Paul and Barnabas on their first missionary journey, Barnabas wanted to give him a second chance on the next missionary journey in Acts 15.

Barnabas was like a fence post to the people he encountered. He encouraged them, supported them, cared for them, and gave them second chances after failure. People were always better off for having been around Barnabas. He was the kind of guy who made you feel better about yourself and gave you the strength to carry on. We all need a Barnabas in our lives. Who among us hasn't had times of spiritual dryness? Who among us hasn't suffered from physical or emotional pain? When you are going through trying times, know who your encouragers are.

As importantly, we all need to be a Barnabas to others. If you look around, you will find many believers who need encouragement. There's so much sadness and hopelessness in the world today. Most people are going through something that is causing fear or anxiety. Maybe they have drifted from Christ, and are like the part of the fence that is far from the post. They have lots of "give" in their spiritual lives. We need to look for opportunities to step into their lives to support and encourage them. It's our responsibility to be the fence post that supports them when they are weak and to remind them of the promises that sustain us. Jesus died for our sins and rose from the dead. Our lives are in His hands, and as believers, our eternal salvation is secure. Those are the fence posts that support our faith.

Reflections:

- Who are the people who serve as your fence posts? List the qualities that make them such good encouragers and try to emulate them.

- Do you have the gift of encouragement? How can you develop it and use it to be a fence post to others?

- Is there someone you can think of right now who could use a little encouragement? What can you do for that person this week?

LEAVING A LEGACY

Matthew 25:21: "His master said to him, 'Well done, good and faithful slave. You were faithful with a few things, I will put you in charge of many things; enter into the joy of your master.'"

BILLY GRAHAM WENT TO BE WITH THE LORD ON FEBRUARY 21, 2018, just nine months short of his 100th birthday. Other than the apostle Paul, I don't know if anyone has ever had a greater impact for Christ. You could perhaps argue for Augustine, Luther, or Calvin. They certainly changed the world and how we think about Christianity. I don't have empirical data, but I doubt anyone ever led more people to saving faith than Billy Graham.

As Christians, rather than mourning his death, we celebrated his amazing life and the fact that he is now with His Lord and Savior. He probably has souls lined up a mile-long waiting to thank him for leading them to

Jesus. My own daughter marks the Billy Graham crusade that we attended in New York City on June 24, 2005, as the moment when she came to Christ when she was only 5. How many placed their faith in Jesus at Billy Graham crusades over the years? How many will those lead to Christ?

What an impact one person can have! We cannot all be Billy Grahams, but who knows whether the person we share Christ with will be the next Billy Graham? I was listening to a sermon recently, and the preacher asked if anyone had ever heard of Edward Kimball. No one had. The preacher went on to tell the story:

Kimball was a Sunday School teacher and was determined to reach his class for Christ. One particular young man tended to fall asleep in class. One day in 1854, Kimball went to see him at the shoe store where he worked. The young man's name was D. L. Moody. Moody accepted Christ and became a famous preacher and evangelist. Moody guest preached in a little chapel pastored by a young man named F.B. Meyer. In his sermon, Moody told a story about a Sunday School teacher who went to every student in his class and led each of them to Christ. That inspired Meyer to evangelism. Meyer later came to America and led a man named J. Wilbur Chapman to accept Christ. Chapman became one of the most effective evangelists of his time. Billy Sunday was a volunteer in his ministry and learned preaching from Chapman. Sunday eventually took over Chapman's ministry and became one of the most effective and dynamic preachers of the 1900's. His evangelism converted thousands.

After hearing Billy Sunday preach in Charlotte, NC, a group of Christians who attended the service set out to reach Charlotte for Christ. They invited an evangelist called Mordecai Ham to come and hold a series of evangelistic meetings in 1932. 16-year old Billy Graham attended one of those meetings and gave his life to Christ. Billy Graham reached millions with the gospel, and it can all be traced back to a humble Sunday school teacher named Edward Kimball. Don't minimize the effect that one humble servant of the Lord can have.

1 Cor. 15:55-57 says, "O death, where is your victory? O death, where is your sting?" The sting of death is sin, and the power of sin is the law; but thanks be to God, who gives us the victory through our Lord Jesus Christ."

Death has no power over believers. It had no power over Billy Graham. It is only a threshold to be crossed. We will hear the words we all long to hear from Jesus Himself, "Well done, good and faithful slave. You were faithful with a few things, I will put you in charge of many things; enter into the joy of your master" (Matthew 25:23). While we wait for that day, let's do our best to ensure that others will hear those words someday too. If we do, we will be part of a legacy that stretches down through the centuries until Christ returns. Who might line up in heaven to thank you?

REFLECTIONS:

- List some people who were instrumental in leading you to faith. Write them a thank you note this week.

- What are some things that keep you from sharing your faith? How could the people who led you to faith help you?

- How could sharing your faith serve to strengthen it?

THINGS THAT DIVIDE

1 Peter 3:8: "To sum up, all of you be harmonious, sympathetic, brotherly, kindhearted, and humble in spirit."

MOLLY AND I WENT TO AN OKLAHOMA UNIVERSITY football game against Texas Tech during the 2019 season. I've been an OU fan since the days of Billy Sims (1978 Heisman trophy winner), and have always wanted to see a game there. Among the sea of rabid OU fans sat a lone Texas Tech Red Raiders fan. He was not shy about his fandom! Every time Tech made a good play, (which was rare), he stood up and turned to face the throngs of fans behind him, and flashed the Texas Tech "guns up" signal while blowing kisses to the crowd. We heckled him mercilessly because his team was down by 30 points or so. But he was funny. He left in the middle of the third quarter to a chorus of boos and jeers.

IN A RELATED STORY, I WAS WALKING ON MY USUAL ROUTE the other morning, wearing an old OU T-shirt with the sleeves cut off. A runner was coming toward me wearing a Texas Longhorns shirt. He said, "We'll see you in two weeks." He was referring to the UT/OU football game known as the Red River rivalry which is played in Dallas during the Texas State Fair every year. A little further on my walk, another runner passed me and flashed me the UT hook 'em horns sign, forefinger and pinky extended.

All of this got me thinking about the things that sports fans. You can't be a Red Sox fan *and* a Yankees fan. You can't be a Giants fan *and* a Cowboys fan. You can't be an OU football *and* a UT football fan. These are hated rivals of each other. A fan has to choose. I respect the UT fans for heckling as they passed me. We both knew OU was going to give UT a beating that upcoming Saturday (They did). I respect the "guns up" Texas Tech fan for being willing to stand alone against a mob of 76,000 OU fans. It was all in fun. He knew Texas Tech had no chance to win, and everyone had a good laugh.

Sometimes though, the things that divide us are much more serious than rooting for our favorite team. You don't need me to tell you how divided our country is right now over so many political and social issues. Every day, we read something new in the headlines about politics, abortion, immigration, health care, gun control, Covid-19, etc. My purpose today is not to address social and political issues, but to address the issues that divide Christians.

I recently had the chance to teach from 1 Peter 1 in our church Sunday School class. In the first two verses,

Peter addressed rich and controversial theological issues including election, foreknowledge, and predestination. As I taught, I thought about how easy it would be for us to divide over these issues. Christians hold different opinions on these weighty matters. I was thankful that even if the people in our class had different theological positions, there was no tension in the class. We can be brothers and sisters in Christ and have differences of opinion on certain issues.

On the other hand, I believe that there are non-negotiables in the Christian faith. For example, evangelical Christians believe in the inerrancy of the Bible. It is God's spoken word. It is infallible and authoritative. From it, we understand that Jesus is eternally God. He is not a created being. He was born of a virgin. He was sinless, and therefore worthy to die in our place, an acceptable sacrifice to God the Father to pay the price that we owe for our sins. He was resurrected in bodily form. He ascended to the Father. He will come again to judge the living and the dead. There is no way to get to heaven apart from faith in Jesus.

These beliefs are currently under attack both from outside the church and inside the church. We expect external challenges. Unbelievers will say that there is no God, or that the Bible is not God's word, or that all roads lead to heaven. But increasingly, the challenge is internal. People who call themselves Christian are jettisoning these essentials of the Christian faith because of cultural pressure. I don't believe that it's possible to be Christian without firmly holding to these central tenets. For example, if the eternality and deity of Jesus are watered down; if Jesus did not die for our sins or was not resurrected; if He's not coming again, then you no longer have Christianity. There are times when Christians have to stand against the mob when it denies the basic truths of Christianity. Peter was preparing his audience in 1 Peter for the suffering they would face for holding onto these truths. We should prepare ourselves for the same.

There are also times when we can agree to disagree. In 1 Peter 3, Peter wrote, "To sum up, all of you be harmonious, sympathetic, brotherly, kindhearted, and humble in spirit." That should always be our attitude. We should not divide over minor differences in theology and practice. May God give us the wisdom to know the difference, grace to live in harmony when possible, and courage to stand alone when necessary.

REFLECTIONS:

- List the essentials of the Christian faith that we must defend. List some of the gray areas that Christians can disagree about without breaking fellowship.

- What might clinging to the essentials of Christianity cost you in the coming months and years? How do you feel about paying that price for your faith?

- How can you learn to be more accepting of those with whom you disagree on non-essentials of the faith?

44

CAN I GET SOME DETAILS?!

Luke 24:50-51: "And He led them out as far as Bethany, and He lifted up His hands and blessed them. While He was blessing them, He parted from them and was carried up into heaven."

I LIKE TO READ HISTORY. I'VE BEEN ON A RECENT KICK, quite by accident, about incidents that occurred in the early 20th century. I recently read a book called *Thunderstruck*, by Erik Larsen, about the invention of the wireless telegraph by Marconi, and how police used it to catch a high-profile murderer named Dr. Harvey Crippen. I've read two books on the exploration of the Amazon jungle. One is called *River of Doubt*, by Candice Millard. She chronicled Theodore Roosevelt's voyage on an uncharted tributary of the Amazon River after he lost the 1912 presidential election. The adventure nearly killed him. The other book is called *The Lost City of Z*, by David Grann, a book about Percy Harrison Fawcett, an explorer who disappeared in the Amazon jungle in 1925 while searching for a fabled lost city of gold. I just finished another book by Candice Millard, called *Hero of the Empire*, about Winston Churchill's escape from a POW camp in the Boer War in South Africa in 1900. Whenever I read history, I am always amazed by the author's meticulous research and the details they unearth and convey to their readers.

I mention all of this because the day of this writing is "Ascension Day," forty days since Easter Sunday, the day Jesus ascended to His Father in heaven. According to scholars, Luke was a first-rate historian and meticulous researcher. In Luke's introduction to his gospel, he told Theophilus that he carefully researched all things before he wrote them down. His sequel to the Gospel of Luke was the book of Acts, in which he detailed the history of the 1st-century church. In both books, Luke referenced Jesus' Ascension. At the end of his gospel, he wrote, "And He led them out as far as Bethany, and He lifted up His hands and blessed them. While He was blessing them, He parted from them and was carried up into heaven." (Luke 24:50-51). In the first chapter of Acts, Luke wrote, "And after He had said these things, He was lifted up while they were looking on, and a cloud received Him out of their sight (Acts 1:9)." That's it! Other than a brief reference to the Ascension at the end of the gospel of Mark, that's all the detail we have about Jesus' Ascension. My wife often jokes that she wishes that women wrote the Bible because they give more details! I agree!

I wish we knew more about the ascension. I wish we had eyewitness accounts from the disciples who were there. (Luke and Mark were not eyewitnesses.) Did Jesus slowly lift off the ground like a hot-air balloon, or did he ascend like a rocket and disappear from view? I want a detailed description of what happened. On this side of heaven, we won't know exactly what the apostles saw. But we do know what the Ascension means. Jesus is alive! He's in heaven now, advocating on behalf of believers before the Father, and defending us against Satan's accusations (1 John 2:1). He's preparing a place for us in heaven (John 14:1-3). He's waiting for the day when He will fulfill all of the promises about His second coming (Rev. 19-21).

Though we may not have all the historical detail we would like, we do have the promise that because He lives, we will live too. And that's good enough for me!

REFLECTIONS:

- There are so few details about the Ascension. What are some of the questions you want answered?

- How does knowing that Jesus is alive today impact your faith?

- How have you learned to live by faith even if not all of your questions are answered?

45

REACHING OUR POTENTIAL

Ephesians 2:10: "For we are his workmanship, created in Christ Jesus for good works, which God prepared beforehand, that we should walk in them."

MY REGULAR WALK TAKES ME THROUGH A CITY PARK WITH softball diamonds on one side and a barren field on the other. As I entered the park this morning, I immediately noticed that something had changed. Yesterday, I barely noticed the field. It's just open space that's typical of Texas. But overnight, it blossomed with beautiful yellow flowers. The unexpected metamorphosis surprised me. I immediately thought about Jesus instructing His apostles not to worry about what they would eat or wear, because if God clothes the lilies of the field, God would He clothe them too. That's surely an apt encouragement in these uncertain times. But the thing I focused on was "potential." Potential is the difference between what something is, and what it may become.

Yesterday, the field was a barren wasteland. I had no idea that it would become a beautiful floral landscape today. It made me think that we are also in a state of "becoming." For those of us who have been saved, we are new creations. Now we have the potential to grow in Christ, to know Him, and serve Him increasingly each day. We should not be complacent on our spiritual walk. We are God's creatures, and He is molding us and shaping us into what He wants us to become. He wants us to realize our full potential. Right now, God may only be planting the seeds in us that will bloom tomorrow through His grace and our cooperation with the Holy Spirit.

When I first started seminary, I would intentionally arrive a minute late to this one class every time because that professor called on students to pray out loud before class. I was too embarrassed to pray in front of others! God has changed me, and all of us who are growing in our faith. Now I pray in front of people just about every day! Paul wrote in Ephesians 2:10: "For we are his workmanship, created in Christ Jesus for good works, which God prepared beforehand, that we should walk in them." God has work for us to do. We may not feel equipped for the work today, but God is constantly working on us to help us to reach our potential in Him. We have to put aside our fears and trust God to continue to work in us.

God wants us to bloom and grow. Like the barren field, we have the potential to be more than we are, to grow in the knowledge of the Lord, and to do the works that God prepared in advance for us to do. The field waits passively to bloom in season, but we are to be active participants in fulfilling God's will for our lives. We need to ask God for the courage to venture out to become all that He wants us to be. By submitting to His will for our lives, God will fulfill His plans for us in ways that will surprise us.

REFLECTIONS:

- What are some of the things in your spiritual journey that were once outside of your comfort zone that are now part of your daily life?

- How does it make you feel that God has already prepared good works for you to do? Can you think of some that you've already done?

- How can you be more aware of the works that God has prepared for you to do?

46

SO, WHAT DID YOU DO THIS WEEKEND?

Psalm 30:5: "Weeping may last for the night, but a shout of joy comes in the morning."

MOST OF THE IDLE CHATTER IN THE WORKPLACE ON Monday morning is about what everyone did over the weekend. You may have talked about the party you went to, or the movie you saw, or the restaurant where you ate. It was the typical, mundane conversation of most Monday mornings as you eased back into the workweek. I like to imagine the workers who showed up at their job site the Monday morning after Jesus' crucifixion. That Monday was anything but routine. When they talked about the events of that weekend, there would have been a ton of talk about Friday and Sunday, but if you read the gospels, there's barely a peep about what happened Saturday, the Jewish Sabbath.

John's gospel doesn't mention the Sabbath between the crucifixion on Friday and resurrection Sunday at all. The other three gospels only make passing reference to it. Matthew 28:1: "Now after the Sabbath…"; Mark 16:1: "When the Sabbath was over…"; Luke 23:56: "And on the Sabbath they rested according to the commandment." Luke is the only gospel writer who reported any action at all, and that action was rest!

Somehow, I don't believe that the Sabbath on that particular weekend was very restful. I'm sure every one of Jesus' followers spent a very long Sabbath grieving Jesus' death. They probably wondered how their Messiah could die. They probably rehashed everything Jesus had said and done during His three years of ministry trying to figure it all out. I'm sure that they were confused, depressed, and without hope.

I've felt like that, and I know you have too. When things don't turn out like we had hoped or expected, we too can feel like Jesus' disciples did on that awful Saturday. But sometimes, as the saying goes, "the darkest hour is just before dawn." God had a plan that Jesus' followers did not understand. They did not know that they would see Jesus alive again the very next day!

If we find ourselves mired in confusion about what God is doing, or if we start to think that some hardship might last forever, that's the time when we have to remember the Saturday of resurrection weekend. When all hope seems lost, God is still in control. Psalm 30:5: "Weeping may last for the night, but a shout of joy comes in the morning."

God always has a plan. We just need to trust Him. Saturday was an unimaginably sad day for Jesus' disciples, but what unspeakable joy awaited them the next day!

They only needed to trust God and wait one more day! The chatter around the water cooler that Monday morning after the resurrection was not about the misery of Saturday, it was about the ecstasy of Sunday. So it is with us. Hang on for one more day. Tomorrow might be the day that God brings inconceivable blessing into your life. God's mercies are new every morning!

REFLECTIONS:

- Describe a difficult season in your life and how God used it for good.

- Discuss a time when you were ready to give up hope but God intervened at just the right time.

47

MEMORIES FROM AN OLD GREEN SHIRT

Joshua 4:9: "Then Joshua set up twelve stones in the middle of the Jordan at the place where the feet of the priests who carried the ark of the covenant were standing, and they are there to this day."

I WENT INTO MY CLOSET TO GET DRESSED AND I CHOSE A hunter green corduroy button-down shirt that I've owned for at least twenty years. Every time I wear it, I think of a picture that Molly took of my daughter Alli and me in an apple orchard in New Jersey, when she was about three years old. Alli still has the picture on a nightstand beside her bed in our house.

It's one of my favorite pictures and memories. It takes me back to the time when our kids were so young and innocent. We were relatively new parents, and our kids were amazed at everything they saw in the world. I love my shirt because it's soft, warm, and comfortable, but it's just a shirt. The picture and the memory are what make the shirt valuable and sentimental to me.

Sometimes we plan to make memories. My father used to record his 5 boys descending the stairs to open presents on Christmas morning. He had an 8MM camera with a light attachment so bright that my retinas are probably still burned. Memories are important to preserve. We hire professional photographers and videographers to record weddings and anniversary parties, so we won't forget. Other times, a smell or a sight can instantly transport us back to a pleasant event from long ago. A picture in an apple orchard can create a recollection that will last a lifetime. We cherish these memories because of their sentimental value, and because when we look back over the years, most days are uneventful and blend together. The uniqueness of a memorable day or moment stands in stark contrast to the regularity and similarity of the rest of our days.

We know from reading the Bible that memories were very important. After God protected Israel from the plague of death on the firstborn of Egypt, God established the Passover feast, so Israel would never forget how God delivered them. When God stopped the Jordan River so the Israelites could cross over to the promised land, Joshua commanded them to set up 12 stones to remind them and all the future generations of Israel what happened there. God intended that the whole nation of Israel remember what He had done.

But sometimes God encounters us personally and creates memories of His goodness that are just for us. I remember going for a walk many years ago when we still lived in New Jersey while I was a new believer. I felt the presence of God with me on that day in a very unique way. There wasn't anything special about the day or the walk, except for God's presence. In 2010, Molly and I were planning to move so I could attend seminary. We were praying for God's guidance. We visited several seminaries, but when we visited the campus in Dallas, we both KNEW at the same time that God wanted us there. I cherish those memories.

When God wants to speak to us, He can do it in spectacular ways, like saving Israel from plagues, or parting rivers. But He can also encourage us in a "still small voice" (NKJV), as He spoke to Elijah in 1 Kings 19 after he ran for his life from wicked Queen Jezebel. God was not in the wind, or the earthquake, or the fire that was all around Elijah that day. God simply whispered. Elijah was a new man armed with the memory of how God spoke to him personally.

There is so much noise in the world that if we aren't expecting to hear from God, we might easily miss Him. But if we are attuned to Him, He may speak to us at any moment and create memories of His presence and His providence that will last a lifetime. He may not part a sea for us, but He may speak in ways that show us that He is present and in control of the circumstances of our lives. God can make an unmemorable day memorable, significant, and sentimental to us just by our awareness of His abiding presence. Our memories of God's presence in little things reassures us that He is with us in all things.

REFLECTIONS:

- Remember and share a time when you were certain of God's presence.

- Joshua commanded the Israelites to set up twelve stones as a memorial to generations. How can you remind future generations of God's providence in your life?

NOTHING REMAINS HIDDEN

Luke 8:17: "For there is nothing hidden that will not be disclosed, and nothing concealed that will not be known or brought out into the open."

IN JANUARY 2020, MAJOR LEAGUE BASEBALL COMPLETED its investigation into allegations that the Houston Astros stole signs during their 2017 World Series championship season. It found compelling evidence that the Astros designed and executed a scheme using the center field TV camera at their home stadium to steal signs from the opposing team's catcher, and relay them to the batter by banging on trash cans. Houston's batters knew whether the pitcher was about to throw a fastball or curveball. MLB punished the Astros by suspending its manager, A.J. Hinch, and general manager, Jeff Luhnow, for a year. The Astros went a step further, firing both Hinch and Luhnow.

THE BENCH COACH FOR THE HOUSTON ASTROS IN 2017 was Alex Cora, who left after that season to manage the Boston Red Sox, who won the World Series in 2018. He was the mastermind of the sign-stealing scheme. The Red Sox didn't wait for MLB to discipline Cora. They suspended him as their manager for the 2020 season the day after the Astros fired Hinch. Carlos Beltran was a member of the Astros in 2017, playing in his final season before retirement. He walked off the field for the last time as a World Series champion, but according to evidence was an active participant in the sign-stealing scandal. The New York Mets hired Beltran as their manager for the 2020 season but fired him in February, a month before the scheduled start of spring training before he ever arrived for spring training or managed a game.

How did this scandal leak? Former Astros pitcher Mike Fiers, playing for the Oakland Athletics the next year disclosed the details to a reporter. From there, it was easy to convict the Astros. There are videos all over You Tube. You can hear the banging of the garbage cans while the pitcher was in his wind-up. It's yet another black eye for baseball, similar to the game-fixing scandal of the Chicago "Black" Sox in 1919, and the more recent steroid and gambling sagas.

The Bible addresses secret conspiracies in Luke 8:17: "For there is nothing hidden that will not be disclosed, and nothing concealed that will not be known or brought out into the open." Those words proved to be true in the wake of the sign-stealing scandal. I love baseball. It hurts my heart that the allegations against the Astros are true. It's bad for baseball, and the people involved. I don't know if Hinch, Cora, or Beltran are Christians, but they didn't act like Christians at the time.

We will often face the temptation to cut corners, bend the rules, or even break them to gain an advantage. It may be at our jobs, on our tax returns, or in other ways. We will only resist temptation by continually "walking in the Spirit." That means a constant awareness of the presence of the Holy Spirit within us, and consistent submission to His will rather than our own. Hinch, Cora, Beltran, and the other Astros yielded to their human desire to win at all costs. Houston's 2017 World Series win is tainted forever. Probably not coincidentally, the Astros won all four of their home games against the Yankees in the American League Championship Series, and 2 of 3 home games against the Dodgers in the World Series. Hinch, Cora, and Beltran will wear this shame like a Scarlet letter for the rest of their lives.

Satan loves it when we stumble and fall, especially if we call ourselves Christians. There is no worse witness for Christ than when a man or woman who professes Jesus as Lord and Savior engages in unethical behavior. The press has a field day, and the body of Christ suffers. We've all done things that we regret. It's part of being sinners. Thank God for Jesus who has paid for our sins. While we live, we don't want to do anything that will damage our witness for Him. We must constantly be on our guard. Satan prowls around like a roaring lion looking for someone to devour (1 Peter 5:8), but greater is He who lives in you than he who lives in the world (1 John 4:4).

NOTE: CORA WAS REINSTATED AS THE RED SOX MANAGER for the 2021 season after his suspension ended.

REFLECTIONS:

- Describe a time when you were tempted to steal, cheat or lie. How did you handle it?

- Why does the world cheer when Christians fail?

- How can Christians guard against hypocritical behavior?

A LEGACY OF PREACHING

2 Timothy 4:2: "Preach the Word."

I HAD LUNCH WITH A GOOD FRIEND WHO ALSO SERVES AS A pastor in a small church. When we finished, he gave me a Christmas gift. It's the original sermon notes written by a preacher you've never heard of who first delivered the sermon in December 1929. The preacher titled the sermon, "Launching Out." The actual content of the sermon is interesting. It's about launching out after failure, from Luke 5:4-5 where Jesus asked Peter to cast out his nets again after he had been fishing all night without success.

Look at the picture of the second page that I've attached. He typed it on an old typewriter on now yellowed and fragile paper. On the second page, the words begin to trail off the bottom of the page because the paper was slipping from the typewriter spool (Kids, ask your parents!). It's covered in handwritten cross-outs and edits. I can imagine him sitting in his office typing and editing. It struck me that since Paul hand-wrote his letters 2000 years ago in candlelit dungeons, humble preachers in small churches have been faithfully preaching the gospel year after year, encouraging the discouraged, and waiting with eager expectation for the Lord's return.

Though technology and culture have changed, preaching God's word has not. This preacher prepared just as I do every week. He typed out his sermon and then furiously and ruthlessly edited it until the moment he delivered it. I can speak from personal experience that we don't always love our sermons. We keep editing to the moment we step into the pulpit. Mercifully, Sunday morning comes so the editing must end and the sermon must be delivered, like it or not. Even then, sometimes the Holy Spirit edits as we preach.

The date of the sermon reminded me that Christmas 1929 was fast approaching, and the stock market crash that caused the Great Depression happened only two months earlier! If we bemoan the fact that we are living in troubling times, imagine what life was like for people who had lost everything they owned only a couple of months earlier. They needed their pastor's encouragement and the reminder that the Lord Jesus loved them.

The pastor who gave me the sermon attached a note that said, "It (the sermon notes) reminds me that we have received the pastoral baton from the previous generation and are in the process of passing it to the next." How true, not only for pastors but for all of us. Jesus commanded us to go and make disciples. Faithful Christians have engaged in that task for 2000 years now.

It's impossible to know the impact that this sermon had on his congregation, but I think the preacher liked it. On the back of the last page, handwritten notes marked when he preached it. He preached it at a church in Massachusetts in November 1942, only 11 months after Pearl Harbor. He preached it again in Belle Meade, Florida in August 1945, just a few months after the war in Europe ended and the month that the US dropped the bombs in Hiroshima and Nagasaki that ended the war in Japan. We lost over 400,000 Americans in the war, and another 671,000 were wounded. How the country needed the gospel during the war, just as much as during the Great Depression.

The lesson is that no matter what is going on in the world, whether it's the Great Depression, World War II, or Covid-19, the gospel is always applicable. It's timeless, relevant, and needed now as much as it was needed then. As that preacher encouraged his flock, allow me to encourage you. No matter what is happening in your life today, Jesus loves you. He gave His life for you. Trust Him with your circumstances. Remember that He is sovereign and that He is good. He has a purpose and a plan. Take comfort in that today!

Reflections:

- How does knowing that Jesus loves you make you feel?

- Commit to praying for your pastor throughout this week, for sermon preparation and to handle God's word accurately.

50

MY QUEST FOR TOILET PAPER
DURING COVID-19

Psalm 19:10: They are more desirable than gold, yes, than much fine gold; Sweeter also than honey and the drippings of the honeycomb."

IN MARCH 1983, WHILE I WAS A SENIOR IN HIGH SCHOOL, A couple of my friends and I wanted concert tickets to one of our favorite bands. Of course, this was long before you could buy concert tickets on the internet. They sold tickets at specific locations, and you had to go there to buy them. One such location was the Garden State Plaza, a giant mall in New Jersey. We drove there with our sleeping bags and provisions for the night. We parked and ran to the door with our stuff. We were the first in line! We nearly froze to death, but as daylight dawned, we started to get excited because soon the doors would open, and the tickets would be ours! What we didn't know was that there was another door on the other side of the mall, where other people were also waiting. They opened our door right on time, but they opened the other door first. The huge crowd from the other door rushed to the front and beat us to the ticket window. We waited all night in the freezing cold and didn't get tickets to the show.

I'm willing to wait in line for concert tickets, but never in my wildest dreams did I think that I would be willing to wait in line for toilet paper. When Covid-19 first hit, you couldn't find any. I went to Kroger at 6 a.m. Zilch. I tried Home Depot and Lowes. Nada. I went to Tom Thumb, but it didn't open until 7. Next was Walmart. I pulled into the parking lot at 6:45 and there was already a line for their 7 a.m. opening. I sat in the car and said to myself, "There's NO WAY I'm standing in line to go to Walmart to buy toilet paper." But as the line grew, do you know what I did? I got in line.

Thankfully, there is only one door at Walmart! When it opened, some people took off running for the paper products in the back row. Others, like me, tried to play it cool, walking casually but quickly toward the back. Two employees guarded the paper products and directed traffic. I was one of the lucky first few. The employees allowed shoppers to take one package of toilet paper and one package of paper towels. I put the treasured items in my cart.

As I shopped for a few other things, I felt mixed emotions. I was so relieved that I had toilet paper! But I noticed other people looking longingly, even jealously at my cart, and I felt a tinge of shame that I had what others wanted. I thought to myself, "Is this what the world has come to during Covid-19, that toilet paper seems to be as valuable as gold?" That thought reminded me of Psalm

19:10: "They (the judgments of the Lord) God's are more desirable than gold, yes, than much fine gold; Sweeter also than honey and the drippings of the honeycomb."

Even though we now have a vaccine, we don't know how much longer Covid-19 will continue to disrupt our world. It could be months or years. What can we cling to in this time of chaos? Like David, we can cling to the word of the Lord. Because we live on this side of the cross and have the New Testament, we can cling to the promise that Jesus made to His disciples in John 14:1-3: "Do not let your heart be troubled; believe in God, believe also in Me. In My Father's house are many dwelling places; if it were not so, I would have told you; for I go to prepare a place for you. If I go and prepare a place for you, I will come again and receive you to Myself, that where I am, *there* you may be also."

Covid-19 has taught us that our lives are a mere breath. We can lose them quickly to an unseen enemy. The economy is volatile. The stock market tumbled at the onset of the virus. Small businesses closed. Thousands of people lost their jobs and their investments. The only solid rock we have is the Lord Jesus. Everything else is sinking sand. That's why we don't panic or allow ourselves to become overcome with fear during this pandemic. God is faithful. He is still on His throne and He is sovereign over Covid-19. He will end this pandemic when He has accomplished His purposes. Our lives will return to normal someday. But even if we should get Covid-19, we do not need to fear. Our eternity as believers is secure. Nothing can separate us from the love of Christ. In heaven, we won't cherish material things like concert tickets or toilet paper. In heaven, we will worship Jesus face to face. We can worship Him today by being faithful, and showing others the love of Christ in this crisis.

REFLECTIONS:

- Describe a time when something material became more important to you than you had ever imagined. (Like toilet paper during a pandemic.)

- How have you learned to cherish the eternal over the material during times of crisis?

- How has Jesus been your peace during a time of great uncertainty?

51

LOVING OTHERS WHILE
SHELTERING IN PLACE

1 John 1:11: Dear friends, since God so loved us, we also ought to love one another. (NIV)

IN THE OPENING SCENE OF "*THE FIDDLER ON THE ROOF*," Tevia sings the famous song, *Tradition*! I know you can hear it in your head now. "Tradition, Tradition!" When we moved to Texas in 2011, we were immediately impressed with how friendly Texans are. Everyone waves and says hello to each other. It's a Texas tradition. Molly and I have been out walking a lot lately while on lockdown and "sheltering in place." We've noticed that people have abandoned the tradition of friendliness. In its place I see suspicion. "Suspicion, Suspicion!" People seem to be suspicious that I may have Covid-19 and that they can catch it from me by making eye contact!

I believe that Covid-19 presents an opportunity, unprecedented in our lifetimes, to show the love of Christ to others. We've had isolated local tragedies like

Hurricane Katrina, Hurricane Harvey, and the earthquake in Haiti. We've even had global pandemics before. The "Spanish flu" in 1918, the H2N2 virus pandemic in 1957-1958, the H3N2 virus in 1968 each killed millions. As recently as 2009, the H1N1 virus ravaged the world killing hundreds of thousands.

Why do I say that this pandemic allows us an opportunity like no other to show the love of Christ? It's because we now live in the information and technology age. As technology continues to advance, we can minister to others in ways that were unimaginable 100 years ago. We can share the gospel, encouraging messages, devotional thoughts, even money, while sitting in front of our computers, sheltering in place. I don't think it's an accident that this pandemic has come along at this time in history. You don't need me to tell you that most of the world has abandoned God. But God has a plan. I pray that one of God's purposes in Covid-19 is to cause revival. If it is, He will do it through Christians who show the love of Christ to a fearful world.

1 John 4:9-11 says this: "This is how God showed his love among us: He sent his one and only Son into the world that we might live through him. This is love: not that we loved God, but that he loved us and sent his Son as an atoning sacrifice for our sins. Dear friends, since God so loved us, we also ought to love one another (NIV).

If you're like me, you're so accustomed to talking to Christians, that you may forget that most people in the world don't trust God's sovereignty and goodness. I've been shocked at the level of fear and panic I've heard from unbelievers. How can we use the resources we have to love one another as God loved us?

Remember that your phone makes phone calls! Call people that you suspect are afraid. Give them assurance and encouragement. Try your hand at writing short devotionals like this one, and send them to your whole email distribution list. Zoom has been a lifesaver in ministry. We started a family Bible study. Now our family that is spread out around the country is meeting weekly to learn about the Bible and pray for each other.

We can invite people to attend church online. Some people are intimidated by walking into a church for the first time. Facebook Live and similar platforms present people with a no-risk opportunity to attend church and hear the gospel. So invite them! We can bring meals, check on the elderly, run errands for people, and do countless other things to show the love of Christ through service. Most of us are probably doing some of these things for our Christian brothers and sisters already. They are the low-hanging fruit of ministry. But if we really want revival, we will have to step out of our comfort zone and start to serve unbelievers too.

I don't want others to look at me with suspicion. I want others to feel the love of Christ through me. I want to help others experience the peace and love of God who sent His Son to die on the cross so that we might live forever in heaven. I want others to know that they don't need to fear Covid-19. If they have trusted in Jesus as their Savior, their place in heaven is secure.

REFLECTIONS:

- Who are the lost and fearful in your sphere of influence?

- How can you use the tools God has given you to show them God's love today?

- What is one thing you can do this week to show God's love to an unbeliever?

52

LOVE ON THE ROCKS

1 Thess. 5:11: "Therefore encourage one another and build one another up, just as you are also doing."

IN THE PREVIOUS DEVOTIONAL, "LOVING OTHERS WHILE Sheltering in Place," I shared some ideas about how we can reach others while sheltering in place during Covid-19 through the technology that is available to us. Technology can be a helpful tool in encouraging others, but it's not necessary. I'm amazed at the many ways creative people can inspire others. On my morning walk today, I passed a rock, no bigger than 2-3 inches long, lying on the sidewalk. I almost didn't see it. In fact, I passed it, and then my brain registered that I had seen something out of the ordinary, so I went back.

Someone named Bob, (not me, another Bob) took the time to glue paper on the rock, and then he wrote an encouraging note on it to people who passed. Bob placed this rock at a strategic intersection where many would see it.

It said, "My name is Bob, I just want you to know that you are special in a good way. Don't let anyone tear you down. Pass this on and put the rock in a different spot." The message is not overtly Christian, but it is encouraging. It shows just a small way that we too can help others who may be stressed and fearful in these troubling times.

Here's another idea. This house is about a mile away from ours. Since the pandemic began, these neighbors have displayed many encouraging messages on their garage door. It's so easy to encourage others if we are willing to make the effort.

Colossians 2:2 says this: "My goal is that they may be encouraged in heart and united in love, so that they may have the full riches of complete understanding, in order that they may know the mystery of God, namely, Christ" (NIV). 1 Thess. 5:11 says this: "Therefore encourage one another and build one another up, just as you are also doing."

. . .

IF TECHNOLOGY INTIMIDATES YOU, THERE ARE STILL MANY ways to help others through this crisis. Be creative and have fun. As Bob and my neighbors encouraged me today, we can encourage others if we look for opportunities.

REFLECTIONS:

- How have you been encouraged by others recently?

- What's one thing you can do this week to encourage someone else?

AFTERWORD

I hope you have enjoyed these devotional messages and would agree that "God is Everywhere!" You can recognize our extraordinary God in the ordinary things in life. Most importantly, it is my prayer that you have learned to love God more through these devotionals. God is beyond comprehension in some ways, but at the same time, He makes Himself known in all that we see so that we have no excuse for unbelief. I hope that these devotionals have helped you see Jesus in all His glory and that you have placed your faith in Him for salvation. If you have, I pray that you have also learned something about how God wants you to live as a follower of Jesus Christ. If you have any questions about how to be saved, or how to follow Him more closely once you've been saved, I would love to hear from you!

If this book helped you and you believe that others could benefit from it too, I would greatly appreciate it if you would leave a brief review wherever you bought this book. Reviews really help authors because they help persuade others that this book is worthy of their investment. Thank you in advance!

You can connect with me on Facebook at Facebook.com/BobJennerich, and Twitter.com/bob_jennerich. Go to my website BobJennerich.com to sign up for my newsletter. There you will also find a link to other books, and more free content, including my blog, and sermons I preached at Grace Redeemer Community Church, Garland, TX.

Free Book!

Type this URL to get a free book called This Is God's Plan?! How We Can Be Certain in Days of Uncertainty.

https://dl.bookfunnel.com/usje1pnyu0

Also Available for sale.

Facing Life's Challenges Head On: How Jesus Gets You Through What You Can't Get Around

ALSO BY BOB JENNERICH

Free Book!

Type this URL to get a free book called This Is God's Plan?! How
We Can Be Certain in Days of Uncertainty.

https://dl.bookfunnel.com/usje1pnyu0

Also Available for sale:

Facing Life's Challenges Head On: How Jesus Gets You Through
What You Can't Get Around

PLEASE LEAVE A BRIEF REVIEW

If this book helped you and you believe that others could benefit from it too, I would greatly appreciate it if you would leave a brief review wherever you bought this book. Reviews really help authors because they help persuade others that this book is worthy of their investment. Thank you in advance!

ABOUT THE AUTHOR

Bob Jennerich was a lawyer in a small law firm in New Jersey when he became a Christian. In 2011, he and his wife, Molly, and their two children, Allison and Brian sold their home in New Jersey and moved to Texas so Bob could attend Dallas Theological Seminary. He accepted the call to become Senior Pastor of Grace Redeemer Community Church in Garland, Texas, in July 2017. Every Sunday he preaches the same gospel that he rejected for so many years. He jokes that if you would have told him 20 years ago that he would be pastoring a church in Texas today, he would have thought that you were crazy.

Bob's passion is to read and study the Bible and teach it to others, so that they too may experience the life transformation that happens when people receive the gospel. The inspiration to write books sprung from his passion to spread the gospel beyond the walls of the church he pastors.

Bob also loves to travel and exercise. He's finished 12 marathons. He's a sports fan, but mostly from the bleachers these days. One of his goals is to go to a game in every major league baseball stadium.